PhotoTripUSA™

LAND OF THE
CANYONS

A Photographer's Guide to Utah and Arizona

by Laurent Martrès

GRAPHIE
INTERNATIONAL, INC.

Published simultaneously in German under the title:
"Im Land der Canyons", ISBN 0-916189-03-1

Published simultaneously in French under the title:
"Au Pays des Canyons", ISBN 0-916189-02-3

A companion photographic CD-ROM is available separately:
"Canyons", ISBN 0-916189-05-8

ACKNOWLEDGEMENTS
All photographs are by the author except where noted.
Cover art: Sioux Bally, Heartstone Arts
Access maps to the regions: Janet Reffert,
by permission of Canyonlands Travel Region and Color Country Travel Region.
Maps to the parks: Patricia C. Joy
English edition edited by Carol Bowdoin Gil

A WORD OF CAUTION
Some of the locations described in this guidebook require travel through remote areas, where foot-paths and 4-wheel drive trails can be difficult to negotiate. Furthermore, the information contained in this guide may have become outdated by the time you read it. Always check conditions locally before venturing out. The author and publisher assume no responsibility if you get lost, stranded, injured or otherwise suffer any kind of mishap as a result of reading the descriptions in this guidebook.

Published by PhotoTrip USA
A division of

GRAPHIE
INTERNATIONAL, INC.

4650 Arrow Hwy. E-3
Montclair, CA 91763
United States
Fax (909) 624-9574
www.phototripusa.com

Printed in the U.S.A.

CONTENTS

APPENDIX

MAPS

FOREWORD

Welcome to this Second Edition of Land of the Canyons — A photographer's Guide to the Colorado Plateau region, covering Southern Utah and Northern Arizona. This new edition includes several new sub-chapters, as well as readers' suggestions.

Choosing this guide shows that we share two common passions: exploring the American West and photography.

With the aid of this book, you'll discover fantastic sites of the Colorado Plateau that are off the beaten track and have largely been ignored by more traditional guidebooks. Most are easily accessible and will provide you with unforgettable images and memories.

Land of the Canyons combines information on numerous sites on the Colorado Plateau with a photographic perspective. In following the recommendations in this guide, you'll visit enchanting, often little known, locations and discover an extraordinary array of journeys that will give free rein to your photographic talents.

This guide supplements other, more traditional travel guides with specialized photographic information. The information is arranged by large geographic areas. Sites whose photographic interest is particularly impressive are listed under these main headings. It also describes how to get there, as well as how and when to get the best shots. It purposely leaves out logistical concerns such as restaurant and hotel accommodations because there are already more than enough books on that subject from which you may choose.

If you're not a photographer, don't close the book just yet! You'll still find lots of travel tips that more traditional guides leave out. This book is not a made-to-order project. On the contrary, it is the product of 20 years of experience discovering the Southwest.

We believe you'll enjoy discovering the infinite photographic possibilities of the Land of the Canyons and make some truly amazing discoveries in the course of following the recommendations of this guide.

Note: an accompanying CD-ROM is available separately, as is the Indian Country Map from the American Automobile Association (AAA)—the best map of the Colorado plateau. The CD-ROM is a Mac/Windows hybrid containing approximately 200 quality color photos, copyright-free, arranged to help you preview the sites—an indispensable part of quality photography.

Formation / Average layer thickness	Era	Where is it found?
Claron formation 180 m	Tertiary	Bryce Canyon
Mancos Shale 1000 m	Cretacean	Capitol Reef
Dakota sandstone 100 m	Cretacean	Capitol Reef
Morrison formation 120 m	Jurassic	Arches, Capitol Reef
Summerville formation 90 m	Jurassic	Goblin Valley, Arches
Curtis sandstone 70 m	Jurassic	Goblin Valley
Entrada sandstone 250 m	Jurassic	Arches, Goblin Valley, Cathedral Valley
Carmel formation 200 m	Jurassic	Capitol Reef, San Rafael Reef
Navajo sandstone 300 m	Jurassic	Zion, Escalante, Arches, Rainbow Br., Capitol Reef
Kayenta formation 100 m	Jurassic	Arches, Island in the Sky
Wingate sandstone 110 m	Triassic	Dead Horse Point, Capitol Reef, Colorado N. M.
Chinle formation 200 m	Triassic	Island in the Sky, Capitol Reef
Moenkopi formation 300 m	Permian	Natural Bridges, Capitol Reef, Fisher Towers
Kaibab limestone 90 m	Permian	Grand Canyon, Capitol Reef
White Rim sandstone 75 m	Permian	Island in the Sky
Cedar Mesa sandstone 360 m	Permian	Natural Bridges, Needles, Maze
Cutler formation 420 m	Permian	Monument Valley, Fisher Towers
Honaker formation 900 m	Pennsylvanian	Shafer Trail, Needles

Sedimentary layers of the Colorado Plateau

INTRODUCTION

A Bit of Geology

What makes the Land of the Canyons so special is their amazing geological origins. The sedimentary layers of the Colorado Plateau were deposited, one after the other, in horizontal strata which were subsequently subjected to erosion by the various elements—wind, rain, and river action—forming fantastic and captivating scenery.

In no other part of the planet does there exist a similar concentration of such singular and varied geologic phenomena. Here the work of erosion manifests itself in such diverse forms as the great depth and enormity of the Grand Canyon, the tight corkscrew shape of Antelope Canyon, the stupendous spans of Arches and Natural Bridges, the incomparable coloration of Bryce Canyon and the fantastic forms in Goblin Valley—all this to our great enjoyment.

This chapter does not pretend to be a course in geology. The author does not have the expertise for that and the reader can no doubt research this in greater depth himself. However, a minimum of geologic knowledge will permit a better understanding of the striking terrain and how it is not merely an inanimate mineral world, but a monumental product of perpetual evolution.

The knowledge of five basic geologic features will enrich your experience of the Land of the Canyons enormously:

❒ the step-like structure of the Colorado Plateau which falls in successive stages towards the southwest;

❒ the various sedimentary layers of the land;

❒ the role of the principal waterways in forming the landscape;

❒ the geographic location of the various mountain chains of the plateau;

❒ and finally, the faults and promontories that fracture and raise the relief of the plateau.

The Grand Staircase

The Grand Staircase starts at the Kaibab Plateau, to the north of the Grand Canyon. The limestone bed of the plateau, 225 million years old, is the first step of the staircase.

The Chocolate Cliffs, a brown color, form the second step. They are found at the south entrance to Zion. The Vermilion Cliffs, of a deep red hue and between 165 and 200 million years old, form the third step. They are found scattered along an imaginary line from St. George to Page. Without a doubt, the most beautiful examples are found along

Route 89A where they appear on the horizon, seen from the viewpoint at Horseshoe Bend.

The White Cliffs, which appear white in strong sunlight but are really an ocher color, are between 135 and 165 million years old. They can be seen along the southern part of Route 89 in the vicinity of Mt. Carmel. The Gray Cliffs, 120 to 135 million years old, form the base of Bryce Canyon and are only visible with great difficulty as they are cliffs in name only. Their soft, friable nature causes them to form an almost worn-out tread on the Grand Staircase. Finally there are the Pink Cliffs, 50 to 60 million years old, that form the top step of the Staircase of which Bryce Canyon is the most representative example.

During your travels across the plateau, you will cross and re-cross these steps of the Grand Staircase. Yovimpai Point, at the end of the Bryce Canyon National Park road allows you to view the Staircase in its entirety from a single vantage point.

Sedimentary Layers

A knowledge, however superficial, of the sedimentary layers that form the plateau will provide a better opportunity to get the most from your visit to the area. All these layers are uncovered, in one place or another. The geology of the Land of the Canyons is like an open book and all you have to do is read it—it couldn't be simpler.

Four formations constitute the majority of those which are most commonly photographed:

❐ the ancient beige Cedar Mesa sandstone of the Permian era forms the spectacular spires of the Needles area of Canyonlands. It is also seen throughout the Natural Bridges area from Blanding to Hite.

❐ the highly polished, deep red Wingate sandstone essentially forms the core of the Island in the Sky and Dead Horse Point. It is also found at Capitol Reef, Little Wild Horse Canyon and the Colorado Natl' Monument.

❐ the ever-present Navajo sandstone can be encountered everywhere on the plateau

Navajo sandstone slickrock

and is best represented by the minarets of Zion, the domes of Capitol Reef and the fantastic slot canyons of Page and the Escalante River.

❒ finally, the superb Entrada sandstone, star of some of the best photos of the American West, finely grained and terra cotta in color which glows a brilliant red in the sunset. It can be found in hard form in Arches, Cathedral Valley, and on the north shore of Glen Canyon, and in a softer, friable form in Goblin Valley or Behind the Rocks.

Rivers

Three principal waterways feed the plateau: the Colorado, the Green and the San Juan rivers. However, many others play an important role in the ecosystem of the Land of the Canyons and merit mention for their esthetic qualities:

❒ the Virgin River, which represents for many their first contact with the Land of the Canyons while following its superb gorge between Las Vegas and St. George and which forms the extraordinary Zion canyon;

❒ the beautiful Sevier River that snakes through the Paunsaugunt Plateau to the west of Bryce Canyon;

❒ the Little Colorado River that feeds into its big brother of the same name and which forms beautiful meanders at the edge of the Grand Canyon;

❒ the Paria River, traversing the Vermilion Cliffs and forming the most spectacular and deepest gorge of the plateau, that of Paria Canyon;

❒ the Escalante River, that drains several watersheds before emptying into Lake Powell and which forms innumerable canyons that would take months to explore;

❒ finally, the Dirty Devil River, which carries waters from

A meander of the Colorado

the Wasatch Plateau and the San Rafael Reef and joins the Colorado River at Hite at the northern end of Lake Powell.

Mountains

At altitudes of 10,000 feet and visible for miles around, the mountains of the Land of the Canyons serve as focal points and enrich the trip as you learn to recognize them. It is possible to measure progress as you travel by observing these mountain chains, which adds an extra dimension to just reading the map. For example, as you descend into Moab in the direction of Natural Bridges, the La Sal Mountains are on your left. A few minutes later, the Abajo Mountains appear directly in front of you and a bit to the right. You'll reach them in the area of Monticello and you leave them behind near Blanding. By the time you reach Natural Bridges National Monument, the Abajos are already well behind and to your right and the Henry Mountains are silhouetted to the left. Traveling the roads of the Land of the Canyons, you will rapidly become familiar with these landmarks, just like a seafarer sailing from port to port.

The La Sal range viewed from Canyonlands

Other Tectonic Phenomena

The geologic structure of the plateau is further complicated by innumerable fractures and upheavals caused by volcanic eruption, earthquakes and other tectonic movements of the earth's crust which have shaped the Land of the Canyons. The Waterpocket Fold, the Moab Fault and the Comb Ridge, to name but a few, illustrate dynamic zones affecting the geology of this region as they alternately raise or lower the sedimentary layers.

Note: You'll find a glossary explaining geologic terminology in the Appendix.

A Bit of Ancient History

In the Land of the Canyons, man is very small, while space and time appear immeasurable. Even multiplied by a hundred, what are a few thousand years of known history in relationship to the slow mineral transformation of this Earth, in successive waves, from volcano to mountain, from river to canyon or from ocean to desert? The ruins of the Fremont and Anasazi cultures, dispersed over the plateau, are eloquent testimony to the vulnerability of the human condition when confronted with implacable nature. In contemplating their abandoned pueblos, sheltered under the immense sandstone cliffs, one cannot help but ponder how fragile their protection really was and what a tenuous hold life has here.

The Fremont and the Anasazi are two ancient, indigenous cultures that are the ancestors of modern Indian tribes. The Fremont populated a geographic zone situated to the north of an imaginary line that passes through Capitol Reef extending to the Great Basin in the west and the Rocky Mountains in the east. The Anasazi inhabited the Four Corners region, so-called because it is the junction of the boundaries of Colorado, New Mexico, Arizona and Utah.

Anasazi means "the ancient ones" in the Navajo language. These ancients disappeared mysteriously around 1250 A.D. The Ute, Navajo, Hopi and other tribes to the south of the Grand Canyon are direct descendants of the Anasazi and Fremont. No one knows with any certainty what caused the disappearance of these ancient ones and their societies. Three theories are frequently advanced: the first presumes that a large meteorite struck the area, blotting out the sun, and rendering the land incapable of growing crops and therefore making it uninhabitable for many years. The second postulates a radical climatic change around the beginning of the 14th century causing increased erosion with the same result—decreased harvests. The third theory rejects

Anasazi pictographs at Newspaper Rock

geophysical causes but is similar to the second in that the consequences were the same. This theory places the responsibility for increased erosion and the disappearance of topsoil on the intensive system of agriculture that the societies practiced which eventually exceeded the capacity of the system to sustain their needs.

Though the answer may elude archeologists, the remains are ample testimony to the well-established social order that was able to assure subsistence and artistic production of great merit. Numerous artifacts discovered on the sites attest to this, in particular the baskets, pottery and fabrics. A visit to Navajo National Monument and the Anasazi and Edge of the Cedars State Parks is strongly recommended for a better understanding of the human history of the Land of the Canyons.

A Bit of Recent History

Explorers, Mormon pioneers, ranchers, cowboys, uranium miners, adventurers....the history of the settlement and exploitation of natural resources in the Land of the Canyons by diverse groups of Europeans is fascinating and the author invites you to discover more about it by reading two seminal works: <u>Mormon Country</u> by Wallace Stegner and <u>Desert Solitaire</u> by Edward Abbey.

<u>Mormon Country</u> by Wallace Stegner is essentially about the Mormon colonization of Utah. This remarkable and impartial document makes easy reading. It would be a shame to travel through Utah without an understanding of this amazing epic of the Mormon pioneers.

<u>Desert Solitaire</u> is a classic by Edward Abbey, a renegade Park Ranger who was simultaneously ultra-liberal and conservative in his views. The author depicts his love of the desert with a fine sensibility, a perfect accompaniment for a trip to Arches and Canyonlands.

Flora and Fauna

The Land of the Canyons is by definition an arid country, limited in types of vegetation and animals. The photographer will not find a great variety of animals. Deer, antelope and rabbits are the mammals most frequently encountered by the roadside and they tend to be most strongly concentrated in the heart of the National Parks and Monuments where they are protected.

There are always mule deer begging for a piece of bread on the main park roadways and near the Visitor Centers; an unfortunate habit reinforced by visitors who want to capture the moment on film, despite numerous official warnings not to feed the wildlife.

Deer and antelope are found in herds from autumn to spring and it is not unusual to see them in groups of about thirty by the side of the road. This is nothing in comparison to the number of deer that it is possible to observe in just an hour's drive to the plains west of the Rocky Mountains.

You will also have the opportunity to observe eagles, falcons, buzzards and the omnipresent ravens. At nighttime, it isn't unusual to spot a great-horned owl in your headlights—an impressive sight.

Snakes, scorpions, spiders? Yes, they are here, but the visitor would have a hard time finding them, especially in the daytime. They present no danger as long as you don't alarm them. It's only necessary that you observe a few precautions when hiking or camping. Special attention should be paid when exploring the narrows or slot canyons that serve as a refuge for these cold blooded creatures during hot summer days.

Seasons

The Land of the Canyons can be visited year-round. Each season possesses its own unique charm and presents various advantages and disadvantages.

The summer is the most crowded time in the best known parks because it is vacation season for the North American hemisphere. Schools and universities are closed during summer. It's the traditional time to "discover the West" in that particular rite of passage common to American families known as "looking for America". The children are packed in the station wagon or motorhome and the family leaves for adventure on the road. In the last few years, foreign visitors *en masse* have also discovered the American West, in organized tour groups or as

Autumn is a perfect season to photograph the Land of the Canyons

individuals, crowding the roads and parks, not to mention the motels. Reservations become indispensable and need to be made before noon to guarantee a place for the night. This can create a serious obstacle to the flexibility of your itinerary by imposing a measure of control on your evening's destination.

The intense heat is not generally a problem in the car or on short walks, but it can become a powerful factor on long hikes. Summer is also the time of frequent afternoon thunderstorms with all the risks they entail, especially when visiting the numerous canyons described in this guide. On the other hand, these storms make for sublime skies, fantastic clarity and spectacular sunsets.

Insects can pose a problem, particularly at the beginning of summer when deerflies and biting gnats or "no-see-ums" will attack your skin relentlessly.

Finally, the days are at their longest and this allows you to cover a lot of ground and see lots of sights. On the other hand, this can considerably limit your photographic opportunities during the day when the sun is high in the sky and your shots will be way too contrasty and without nuance.

Autumn is without doubt the best time to discover the Land of the Canyons. It's still warm, but the heat is less ferocious. The days are still long, but less grueling. The students and a large part of the population have returned to work after the Labor Day holiday. The motels empty out and reservations are not as necessary. Prices lower to a reasonable level, the parks are not as congested and parking near the panoramic vistas no longer requires you to drive around for half an hour to find a spot. Also, insects will not make your life miscrable. October and November are absolutely marvelous in Zion or Capitol Reef as the foliage changes and a new, multi-colored palette of ochers and reds appears with a less-defined illumination than in summer. Strong rains are relatively rare, but at high altitude locations such as Cedar Breaks or Bryce, snow is possible.

Winter is the off-season and offers exceptional possibilities for a visitor to the American West to enjoy the surrounding tranquillity at incredibly low prices. With a bit of care to dress warmly, the dry cold is not disagreeable, though it can make camping less attractive. The only real inconveniences are the cloudy periods when the snow or rain can last two or three days. However, a snowfall in Bryce can be an absolutely magical experience when, with these alternate periods of beautiful weather, the air attains an unequaled purity and the sky is an intense blue. Unobstructed views such as those one sees in Canyonlands or the Grand Canyon, to give but two examples, reveal extraordinary distances when there is no pollution, as is rarely the case in the Grand Canyon in summer. Animals descend from the mountains and are frequently and easily observed in the valleys. The only major inconvenience is that certain sites become inaccessible, particularly the North Rim of the Grand Canyon, Cedar Breaks, the Narrows of the Virgin and sometimes the trails of Bryce (at least without adequate equipment, for these last two).

Spring is a magnificent season. The peaks are still snowbound, greenery is sprouting and the trees are leafing out. The rivers and waterfalls are at their highest, the days are getting longer and the prices are still not as expensive as during the height of the season. However, the weather is still

The Zion Narrows offer plenty of solitude in Winter

unstable and precipitation is frequent. Insects can also present a great nuisance. No-see-ums, fond of blood and penetrating everything, and aggressive deerflies are to be found along the water courses and in the washes.

Some Photographic Advice

Prints or slides? It's without doubt the question that pops up the most in discussions on CompuServe's Photography Forum, of which the author is a moderator. It is therefore of some interest to raise it here. The bottom line is that more and more photographers think that it is possible to obtain excellent results using both.

In the past few years, print film has largely overcome the handicap of poor quality that it had compared with positive film. Modern emulsions, incorporating micro granulation technology, are remarkable and perfectly suited to small automatic cameras equipped with slow zoom lenses, used without a tripod during a pleasure trip. The capacity of negative film to capture nuances and forgive exposure errors can be very useful in many instances. That said, the quality of your prints will ultimately depend in large part on your choice of photo lab. Concerning film, the author recommends a speed of 400 or 800 ISO. The grain on these new, fast emulsions is totally invisible on a standard format print, and barely noticeable on large format enlargements. This speed advantage is crucial when working without a tripod, especially in the slot canyons where it becomes possible to work with considerably shorter speeds. Also, exposure can easily be corrected in the lab during the printing process. If you are not satisfied with the results, you can ask for a reprint accentuating red, yellow or orange, over or under exposing the print to reduce shadows and bring out detail. Finally, the ease with which you can show your prints to friends and family is self evident.

Color slides, on the other hand, provide high quality results and are more true to life but impose many more constraints than color negative film. In the first place, correct exposure is absolutely critical. This effectively excludes the use of color transparency film in point & shoot cameras that do not allow for manual exposure compensation. In addition, you lose at least one stop by comparison to the exposure range of negative film and you must constantly concern yourself with keeping the contrast between light and dark areas to a minimum. Finally, although slow color transparency emulsions have almost non-existent grain, this becomes very present at film speeds above 200 ISO. All these factors

The Land of the Canyons is prime territory for nature abstracts

make it necessary, in a number of circumstances, particularly in the narrows and slot canyons, to use a tripod if you want to take slides. You must admit this would be a nuisance for what is supposed to be a pleasure trip.

Ninety-five percent of professional photographers use slide film, however, this is largely dictated by the needs of magazine editors more than personal choice. Slides can be immediately examined on a light box and, with a good loupe, the editor can judge the qualities and faults of a first generation image. A printed photo is already a second generation image, which makes it impossible to ascertain how it will reproduce in a magazine. However, these considerations need not concern the amateur. For him, choice of film is essentially a matter of taste and the effort he is ready to put out to show his photos.

Some additional remarks concerning photography in slot canyons and narrows are in order. The range of perception of film is greatly limited in comparison with the human eye and it is impossible to reproduce on film all the nuances

Photographing slot canyons may involve some very messy aspects

that we perceive. In the case of slot canyons, the task consists of perfectly exposing the part that most interests you within the limitations of the film range. This can be achieved in two ways: by selectively choosing your composition to avoid too many highlights and minimizing areas in deep shadow, otherwise these shadows risk appearing completely black, especially on a slide (note that you should never photograph light directly hitting a canyon wall); or by making an intelligent compromise between the various spot measurements obtained on those parts of the wall for which you want to preserve detail.

If your compositions include a close subject, it is important to work with the smallest possible aperture (i.e. the highest settings such as f/16 or f/22) to guarantee maximum depth of field. In essence, except under particular circumstances where you want to isolate a detail from an indistinct background, it is very disappointing to view a photo in which some parts are not razor-sharp. This becomes even worse if you enlarge the photo.

If you use an autofocus reflex camera, it is preferable to work with the manual focusing option and to set the distance not as a function of exact focus when viewed through the lens, but by using the depth-of-field marks of your lens creatively to maximize sharpness within the particular range of distance pertaining to your shot. Unfortunately many modern lenses, particularly the zooms, lack depth of field marks and it is often necessary to improvise.

Concerning exposure, if you are working with slides and wish to obtain the best results, take five different shots at 1/2 stop intervals on either side of the setting you think is correct. In the case of negative film, this is useless since the density of the highlights and shadows can easily be altered during the printing process. Negative film tolerates up to 2 stops of overexposure fairly well, but does poorly with underexposure. If you are a perfectionist, you can always take a second shot with one stop of overexposure—it is useless to try more.

There is also a somewhat complex technique consisting of pre-exposing an 18% gray card before taking the actual shot on the same frame. This has the effect of reducing contrast and bringing out more detail in the shadow areas. As you can imagine, this is rather cumbersome to implement within the framework of a pleasure trip.

Attention should also be paid to the reciprocity failure characteristics of your film, especially if you are using a tripod and slow film. With exposures of several seconds, certain slide films display a tendency towards incorrect exposure and you risk having underexposed shots. There are reciprocity failure tables for the major brands of film on the market. Unless you are talking of exposures of four seconds or more, you shouldn't have to worry about this.

Cascades offer great photographic opportunities

The Great White Throne from Angel's Landing (Photo by Scott Walton)

Chapter 1
ZION NATIONAL PARK

Located at the head of the line for visitors coming from Los Angeles and Las Vegas, Zion is frequently the first national park visited by travelers making the "Grand Circle" of national parks in the American West. It's a spectacular introduction to the discovery of the Colorado plateau.

For the visitor with very little time, the park consists of two parts: the canyon and the plateau.

The canyon is deeply cut (between 2,000 and 2,500 feet), which doesn't make for easy photography because of the great contrast between the sunlit summits and the valley plunged in deep shadow. If you are visiting by car, you can travel with the sun as it crosses the valley and harvest a great crop of photos. If you travel by motorhome, you should note that there are parking restrictions in the canyon and you will need an escort to go through the tunnel. Finally, there is talk of implementing a mandatory shuttle service around the year 2000 to reduce the congestion and pollution in the canyon's interior.

If possible, the most interesting way to arrive in Zion is by way of the plateau since the views are particularly spectacular coming from Mt. Carmel. It's a shame to do it in reverse. In addition, illumination is best in the morning at the principle viewpoints of the plateau.

Rock formation typical of the Zion plateau (Photo by Steve Berlin)

If you follow this advice, you have two possibilities: visit Zion at the end of your "Grand Circle" or make a detour through Kanab. In practice, spending the night at Kanab is very feasible if you leave from Los Angeles in the morning. If you leave from Las Vegas, you are only three hours from Zion and you'll be hard pressed to resist the attraction of starting from the canyon.

We begin our visit at the plateau, but the choice is up to you. In any case, you will not be disappointed by the universe of Zion.

The Zion Plateau

All of the southwest area of the park, on Scenic Byway 9 between the east entrance and the tunnel, is absolutely spectacular and offers numerous photographic possibilities. It is without doubt one of the most fantastic landscapes you'll encounter. The rock walls, some white, some red, possess extraordinary rounded forms, whereas the summits are ornamented like minarets. A sculptural sensuality emanates from this topography that defies the imagination. The ground switches from polished to checkered within a very short space. Stone tumuli scorched raw by the wind, burst forth here and there from a ground alternately smooth and lined. It's an incongruous landscape, kneaded, molded and painted as if by some crazy baker.

Checkerboard Mesa

A short distance from the entrance station, you'll find the viewpoint of Checkerboard Mesa, one of the most celebrated views in Zion. The prow of the mesa is inclined at a 60° angle and is striated like a baguette fresh out of the oven. Checkerboard Mesa appears best in mid-morning until the beginning of the afternoon, with the sun on the left. If you come from the valley, you will be against the sun after noontime. The view of Checkerboard Mesa is a classic and it's difficult to take an original shot even by changing the viewing angle. It is mostly the unusual checkerboarding of the Mesa, more than its own beauty, which makes for the interest in this photo.

Checkerboard Mesa in Winter

The Canyon Overlook Panorama

Coming from Mt. Carmel, you reach this viewpoint from a parking spot located just before the entrance to the tunnel. The trail is about a mile long, round trip, and a bit difficult in spots. The viewpoint overhangs the Great Arch—which is in fact an alcove—that you can see

The Canyon Overlook panorama is a good morning shot

and photograph while descending the switchbacks leading into the valley. From this often windy viewpoint, you'll gain a superb view of the entrance to Zion Canyon. Pine Creek and the switchbacks of the main road are visible below, but they only become sunlit in mid-morning during the summer and the middle of the day in winter. Very early in the morning, you can isolate the West Temple and the Towers of the Virgin with a short, 85 to 100 mm, telephoto by concentrating on the golden rock face and eliminating the problematic shadow areas. By the end of the morning, the walls are basking in direct sunlight and have lost their relief. Of the park's three high observation points (Angel's Landing and Observation Point are the other two) this one is by far the most accessible, but unfortunately it's also the least spectacular.

The Towers of the Virgin

At sunrise, this is the most beautiful panorama in Zion. If you love beautiful lights on rock walls, you won't be disappointed. The sun penetrates the valley through the Pine Canyon fault and bathes the summits of the temples in a warm gold light. Station yourself directly behind the Visitor Center and mount a 35 mm lens. This will allow a tight framing of the West Temple, the Sundial, the Temple of the Virgin and the Altar of Sacrifice and keep the shadowy zone at the bottom of the photo to a minimum. A graduated neutral density filter is strongly recommended to maintain detail in the shadowy zone and to conserve the vibrant red and gold color of the high walls. You'll have a good thirty minutes before the sunrays irradiate the summits with so much light that the shot gets lost. If you are spending the night close by, in Springdale or in Zion, this sunrise vista is a must.

The Towers of the Virgin from behind the Visitor Center

The Court Of The Patriarchs

Zion Canyon reveals all its splendor as the sun climbs over the surrounding peaks and your first stop should be to view the Court of the Patriarchs. You'll get the best results between sunrise and mid-morning. At the end of a short trail, you arrive at an unrestricted viewpoint where you can photograph the Patriarchs with a wide angle lens. A

The Three Patriarchs

24mm is essential to include all three summits, but you can also get equally good results with a 28 or even a 35 mm, though you won't be able to fit in more than two of the Patriarchs. Finally, a short telephoto lens will let you isolate them individually.

Emerald Pools and Weeping Rock

These two sites are not quite on the same scale as the others in the canyon. If you are pressed for time and have to make a choice, you can eliminate them without regret.

The Emerald Pools, especially the lower one, are heavily visited and can be reached by a trail of a little over a mile, round trip, from the Zion Lodge. Or you can take one of about 2 miles, round trip, from the Grotto parking lot. It's usually easier to find a parking spot at the Lodge in season. The attraction of this spot rests in the water droplets raining on you from the walls. There are also three lovely little cascades nearby. In summer, you'll find it quite pleasant to rest under the maple trees and bask in the fine mist of water enveloping you, though the photographic interest here is limited.

It's much the same at Weeping Rock. You pass behind a curtain of water droplets falling from the rock face, the end result of a two-year voyage through the porous rock. Twenty minutes should be enough for a brief visit.

The Temple of Sinawava

This remarkable area, located at the end of Zion Canyon, is one of those special spots that evokes a mystical and spiritual connection with nature. The happy traveler, intoxicated by the succession and variety of the panoramas of Canyon Overlook, the Towers, the Patriarchs and brief glimpses of the Great White Throne attains a sort of nirvana when reaching the Temple of Sinawava. The Pulpit rises in the middle of a cove formed by the river. As a result of the twists and turns of the canyon, its lighting is unfortunately mediocre in the morning and evening but by pacing yourself along the Scenic Drive you can time your arrival for early afternoon, which is the best time to photograph it.

Further on, the 1 mile-long surfaced Riverside Trail (unfortunately as crowded as Los Angeles freeways at rush hour) leads to the Gateway to the Narrows, the entrance to the Virgin River Narrows. The trail, which follows the bank of the Virgin River, offers magnificent views in the spring and early summer, as well as later in autumn when the foliage changes color. In the opinion of the author, this walk is not a necessity if you are pressed for time, unless you have definite plans to hike the Narrows.

The Virgin Narrows

It's an unforgettable memory to go up the Virgin Narrows for an hour or so or until you reach the confluence with Orderville Canyon. The principal interest of the narrows, compared to other more accessible or perhaps more photogenic locations, resides in the fact that you are almost constantly immersed in the Virgin River, often up to your knees and sometimes higher. Out of season, the Virgin River is glacially cold or its water level is too high, so it is recommended that you make this journey during summer. Unfortunately, if you do, you won't be alone and will also run the risk of flash flooding. At the entrance to the Narrows, there is a sign post warning of the potential risks of flash floods and rating the danger for the day. Permits are not required for day-hikers. The

The author exploring the Narrows

Park service strictly forbids walking the narrows on days when a storm is threatening. You can rent a dry suit, as well as Neoprene socks and canyoneering shoes to make the experience safer and more enjoyable, but a good pair of stiff hiking boots with firm ankle support will also do an excellent job. You should also consider carrying a walking stick to probe the river bed for treacherous rocks or holes and to keep your balance if the current is strong. Out of season, this equipment becomes absolutely indispensable. (Check under the chapter on Resources in the Appendix.)

The upper Narrows (Photo by Gene Mezereny)

Walking the Virgin Narrows can be a real pleasure. Nevertheless, if this seems a bit too much or you don't feel ready to walk in cold water, don't despair. Later in the book, the author will propose four relatively easy walks of similar interest and originality; two inside narrows (see Buckskin Gulch and Coyote Gulch) and two in slot canyons (see Peek-a-Boo and Little Wild Horse Canyon). Don't miss reading the chapters concerning these extraordinary and little known sites. Scores of visitors crowd the Zion Narrows while adventures and photographic possibilities abound elsewhere.

The complete descent of the Virgin Narrows requires two full days as well as preparations and logistics beyond the scope of this book.

Photo advice: from a photographic standpoint, one of the unique features of the Narrows of the Virgin River is the chance to take photos of yourself or your friends wading in the water, fording the narrows. To eliminate problems, a fast film is needed as the Narrows are very shady and it would be cumbersome to bring a tripod, unless you are very serious about your photography. ISO 400 to 800 is perfect and this is a good place to use color negative film. The new emulsions have a microscopic grain which is barely discernible in enlargements. The resolution is excellent, contrast is relatively easy and perfect for this type of situation and the latitude of exposure is very large. Save the slide film for other narrows where you will be able to take advantage of different compositions.

If you have at your disposal a small automatic camera, bring it in preference to a more expensive one. Just remove it from your pocket when an opportunity presents itself and the zoom will let you take excellent pictures of people. If all you have is a reflex camera, protect it in an airtight plastic bag. You will have to walk over slick rocks and it's easy to take a spill. The author strongly recommends against taking expensive medium or large format equipment into the Narrows.

Time required: three to four hours round trip to reach the junction of Orderville Canyon (the final destination for 90% of the visitors making the journey), but an hour will suffice to get a glimpse of the place and take some people shots if you are in a hurry.

The Great White Throne

It's preferable to see the Great White Throne on your return from the Temple of Sinawava, as you'll have to cut across traffic if you do it first. It is without doubt one of the most recognizable symbols of Zion. Unfortunately, it does not allow itself to be photographed as easily as you would like. There are two vantage points, both situated on the right side of the road returning from the Temple of Sinawava. The first allows a rectangular framing of the throne between two walls of the canyon, which is quite mediocre. The second vantage point offers a more unobstructed view and much more leeway to play with the light, whether you keep to the perfectly satisfactory view from the road or descend to the bank of the Virgin River. The best lighting is in the middle of the afternoon. Too early in the day, the canyon is shrouded in shadow and later in the evening it is backlit.

The Great White Throne from the canyon

Zion Canyon from Angel's Landing

Angel's Landing

Because of its central location, this is the most beautiful view of Zion Canyon but to access it will require excellent physical condition and a lot of exertion. Above all, heights must not make you dizzy. You'll start your ascent from the Grotto parking lot, following the extremely steep switchbacks of the West Rim Trail before reaching the welcome shade of Refrigerator Canyon. Scaling another series of switchbacks, you arrive at the first viewpoint, Scout Lookout, where you have an exceptional and very steep view of the upper part of the Canyon's meanders as well as of the Temple of Sinawava. The last five hundred yards require a lot of effort as you painstakingly move forward up a stunning trail which is more of a rock flank. Chains are anchored in the rock for use as handholds. The round trip from the Grotto is about 5 miles. The vista from the top of Angel's Landing is sensational and well worth the effort. You can see the entrance to Zion Canyon opening up to the right, while in the center you get a breathtaking view of the Great White Throne. To the left, the canyon meanders toward the Temple of Sinawava.

Photo advice: ascend in late afternoon to get the best lighting. You'll need a 24mm to frame both the Great White Throne and the Canyon.

Time required: 3 hours round trip. Caution: this trail is not recommended for anyone in poor physical condition or prone to vertigo. If you are in doubt as to your physical condition, skip it, as you'll have to turn back when you arrive at the beginning of the chains without having caught a glimpse of the view.

Kolob Canyon Viewpoint

The Kolob section of Zion is rather remote from the Canyon and many travelers pressed for time pass it up. That's a shame because the valley that follows the road towards Cedar City is very pretty. Also, the road through the park only runs about 6 miles before reaching the Kolob Canyon Viewpoint, making it a very short trip. All along the route, the view of the impressive red rock walls is remarkable. The

The view from the upper vista point

detour is worthwhile if you decide to go up to Bryce by way of Cedar Breaks. But don't let it cause you to miss the road from Zion to Mt. Carmel, allowing you to cross the plateau. If you have to choose, the plateau should be the first priority.

Getting there: use Interstate 15 from St. George or Cedar City. This section of the park is frequently closed in winter.

Photo advice: the best time is late afternoon.

Time required: 1 hour round trip from Interstate 15.

Double Arch Alcove

This is a very scenic and highly recommended hike to a fantastic photographic location: a vast grotto-like alcove, topped by two closed arches carved in a 2000 feet cliff. The trail is extremely easy and suitable for families with young children. It is only 2,7 miles o/w to Double Arch Alcove on a mostly flat trail. You will cross Taylor Creek numerous times, but none of the crossings presents a challenge; in fact, you even end-up walking in the shallow creek bed toward the end of the hike, which is a lot of fun.

The canyon walls and vegetation are splendid all along the trail and you'll pass two old cabins on your way. There is a patch of intense green grass at the bottom of the alcove which contrasts beautifully with

Double Arch Alcove towers over Taylor Creek

the red rock. In the fall, you'll get the benefit of intense yellows and reds to complement your photos. Some very large pines and spruce trees grow above the first and second alcoves, adding a touch of green to your composition.

Getting there: the trailhead is only 3 miles from the Kolob Section entrance on I-15 between St. George or Cedar City. This section of the park is frequently closed in winter.

Photo advice: a 24mm or 28mm works best to encompass the entire rock wall including some vegetation at the bottom, the alcove and the two arches. Best photographed around midday under the reflected light from the opposite rock wall, which gives the alcove a fantastic orange and red glow.

Time required: 3 hours round trip.

Crossing Zion by way of the Kolob Terraces

For those with time and a thirst for adventure and hidden corners, it's possible to cross Zion from north to south in a high-clearance or 4WD vehicle. You can start either from Cedar City or Kanaraville to the north or from Virgin to the south. The road is known as the Kolob Reservoir Road and is classified as a Scenic Backway. The northern part of the route, unpaved and in very poor repair, crosses privately-owned land on the Kolob Plateau. It's difficult to follow because of tracks left by the pickups of local ranchers, but with a bit of close attention you can quickly locate the right one going to Kolob Reservoir by way of Blue Spring Reservoir and enter the park at Lava Point. The main attraction of this foray into the high country is in crossing the semi-alpine landscape and the solitude that one is sure to encounter there.

Getting there: take the Kanaraville exit on I-15, follow the Kanaraville signs south until you find the trail on your left about a mile from the off ramp, or from Virgin simply follow the Scenic Backway sign.

Getting to Zion

Photo advice: in the early evening, you'll have superb views of the Kolob Terraces lit by the setting sun with magnificent tall grasses in the foreground. Fantastic views abound between mile 8 and 15 from Virgin.

Time required: 3 hours. Make sure your vehicle is in excellent running condition and take supplies. The author drove the 45 mile distance without encountering another vehicle. The road is closed by snow in winter.

The Subway

This is a fantastic location, but also a very hard hike, and if you are thinking of taking heavy photographic equipment, you'd better think twice, because you will feel it all the way and back. However, the surreal sight that awaits you at the end of the journey makes it all worth it.

The Subway is a narrow canyon that has been carved tunnel-like fashion by the waters of North Creek. In one curve made by the river, it feels like you are in a tunnel, except for a narrow opening at the top. North creek gently winds its way on the polished red rock under your

Magical pools and cascades of the Subway

feet, flowing over pools of azure and green; small cascades trickle down pour-offs and choke stones further up. The absence of light reinforces the crypt-like feeling of the Subway. It is a very haunting place indeed.

You'll need a permit to visit the Subway. It is not too difficult to come by because the N.P.S. issues up to 50 of them each day. You can apply for your permit at the backcountry desk of the Visitor Center, up to two weeks prior to your visit. Overnight camping is no longer permitted inside the canyon. In summer, you might find serious competition for the permits from adventurous young people intent on a day of wading and rappelling. In other seasons, crowds are more sparse and on a cold or overcast day you may well be the only soul venturing into the canyon. The author strongly recommends that you go with an outfitter (refer to the Resources chapter) because of the difficulty of the trail and the possibility of injury.

Photo advice: regardless of the format you shoot, you will need a sturdy tripod because the light is extremely dim and you'll find yourself working with very long pauses: 8 to 30 seconds if you shoot slow film and want maximum depth of field. This is prime territory for reciprocity failure and you had better know the characteristics of your film and how it reacts to cool dim light. A warming filter would certainly help warm things up a bit, although the very cold blue light creates a very ethereal effect.

Getting there: You can reach the Subway from two different trailheads. The easiest way, at least for a photographer carrying equipment, is to go from "the bottom", a trailhead located about 8 miles north of the Kolob Terraces Scenic Byway turnoff in the town of Virgin. To call this entry "the bottom" is a figure of speech because after only half a mile of flat walking, you must negotiate a difficult descent down a steep gully. A walking stick or pair of trekking poles will make

The tunnel-like entrance of the Subway

this descent as well as the whole day much easier. Once you reach the bottom, you follow the creek up the best you can, crossing and re-crossing many times. Sometimes there is a visible trail, at other times there is none. It will be a challenge to keep your feet dry all the way but it can be done by detouring over the bigger boulders and crossing with the help of trekking poles. This "easy" way is a compromise which allows you to see only the lower part of the Subway, albeit the most spectacular one.

The other way, certainly more fun and adventurous, is to come from "the top", parking at the Wildcat Canyon trailhead and following the Great West Canyon for a while until it meets North Creek. From there, you'll need to rappel your way down several cascades and choke stones. You'll need a partner or two to make this trip safe and it is not recommended to take heavy equipment on this one. From the Subway, you can either retrace your steps or continue all the way to "the bottom" if you have arranged a car shuttle.

Time required: a whole day.

AROUND ZION

The Smithonian Butte

An excellent way to get to Zion is by using the nine mile long Smithonian Butte Scenic Backway. Seen from Route 89 coming from Fredonia, the scenery is magnificent in all seasons with the Canaan Mountains to the east and the tall grass prairie in the foreground. However, it's on the Scenic Backway itself, going toward Rockville, that a surprise awaits you with an extraordinary view of the entrance to Zion Canyon. From the mesa, you can clearly see the Watchman to the right of the canyon entrance and the Towers of the Virgin to the left. Just before reaching Rockville, a short detour leads to Grafton, a turn-of-the-century ghost town resembling those in movie Westerns.

Getting there: on Route 89 coming from Fredonia or from Hurricane, the road begins about 15 miles to the east of Hurricane and comes out at Rockville, a mere 4 miles from the west entrance to Zion. It is marked by a small Scenic Byway sign. The otherwise excellent road deteriorates rapidly as it plunges toward Rockville and you'll have to exercise caution. Coming from Rockville, the road is not marked. You'll need to make a turn at a small sign marked Bridge Street from the main road in order to catch it.

Photo advice: from the highest point on the Smithonian Butte Backway, reached after about four miles off Route 89, the angle is just perfect for an early morning or late afternoon shot of Zion. The serrated ridge of the Smithonian Butte comes into view at this spot, looking much like the backbone of a dinosaur.

Time required: 45 minute detour off the main road.

Coral Pink Sand Dunes State Park

This Utah State Park is really worth a detour, at dawn or sundown, if you happen to be in the vicinity. As its name indicates, these are sand dunes of a beautiful strong ocher tint. The extremely fine sand—Navajo sandstone ground and sifted by wind over and over again—becomes an extraordinary coral pink in the setting sun. The dunes were formed by hot air currents coming from the south and accelerating as they pass through Moccasin Gap, seen to the southwest of the viewpoint. These currents lose their speed when coming in contact with cold air masses forming above the Grand Staircase region and deposit sand in this area.

The dunes are spread out over a relatively small area, which makes it easy on the hiker or photographer. From the parking lot, you can quickly get to the summit of the two main dunes, which are not more than 40 feet tall. The surroundings are not exactly exceptional, but the White Cliffs to the north and the Vermilion Cliffs to the south allow you to add some depth to these superb dunes. This park should not be missed if you are traveling with children.

Getting there: the park is located about 12 miles from Mt. Carmel on the Ponderosa/Coral Pink Sand Dunes Scenic Backway. Coming from Zion or Bryce, leave Route 89 about 3.5 miles south of Mt. Carmel Junction. If coming from Kanab, exit Route 89 about 8 miles north of Kanab. Signs mark the two routes which are fully paved, except for a small section to the south. Watch out for livestock as they are free to roam along this route.

Photo advice: the interest here is as much along the order of macrophotography than landscapes. Motifs created by the wind and the vegetation stand out from an interesting pink background. Out of season, you can get fantastic panoramic views of the dunes without any trace of footprints on their summits—something you'll be hard pressed to achieve in Death Valley or Colorado's Great Sand Dunes. Contrary to lighter-colored sand dunes, like those of Death Valley, it is not necessary to compensate by overexposing. A normal exposure will preserve the shadows and reliefs of the motifs on the sand as well as the beautiful ocher color. Try to be in position on the dunes at Sunset; you'll be treated to an unbelievably pink glow turning into a dramatic red during a brief but miraculous last minute before the sun disappears behind the horizon.

Time required: 1 and 1/2 to 3 hours.

Beautiful wind sculpted patterns in the Coral Pink sand

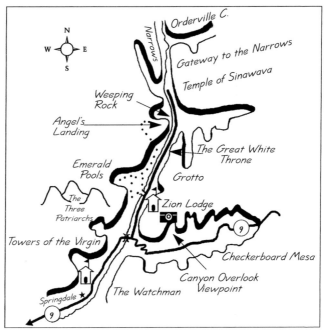

Zion canyon

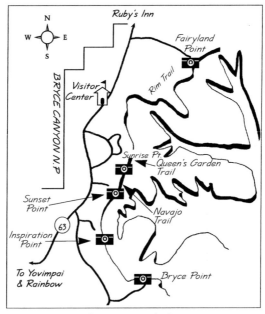

The Bryce Amphitheater

Bryce Amphitheater from Sunset Point

Chapter 2
BRYCE CANYON NATIONAL PARK

Bryce Canyon, along with Arches, is the park preferred by the majority of visitors to the Land of the Canyons, especially foreign visitors, who come from the four corners of the globe to admire it. The whole world, consequently, has seen images of Bryce and the name immediately invokes a geological phenomenon bordering on the supernatural. A case in point: a French software application generating virtual landscapes is named after this park and its publisher didn't have to explain the choice of name to the public. Happily or unhappily, its proximity to Los Angeles and Las Vegas makes access easy. As a result, there is a strong concentration of Disney-like tourist attractions around the amphitheater area. This phenomenon is reinforced by the presence of the sprawling Ruby's Inn complex located at the park entrance right in the middle of the desert-like Sevier Plateau. It's unlikely that you'll find solitude or spiritual communion with the environment at Bryce, but you are sure to find a landscape that will hold you in an hypnotic trance the first time you lay eyes on it. It's a landscape filled with weird and incredible formations combined with remarkable nuances of light and saturated with color. It's understandable that visitors are attracted to the spot.

Sunrise and Sunset Viewpoints

Sunset Point is unarguably the best spot to admire and photograph Bryce Canyon. It's also the most popular and you won't be alone. The view on both sides is excellent, looking towards Sunrise Point on the left or Inspiration Point and Bryce Point on the right. The Silent City is set back from the first viewpoint to the right of the parking lot. Mornings and late afternoons are excellent for photography. If your time is limited, Sunset Point is the best place to catch Bryce in all its glory.

Sunrise Viewpoint is the first stop on your way to the Visitor Center. The formations are not as densely packed as those at Sunset Viewpoint, but they are just as lovely. It's easier to isolate individual formations from Sunrise Point with a short telephoto lens. However, Sunset Viewpoint offers a more spectacular panorama on both sides, whether you aim at Sunrise Viewpoint or Inspiration and Bryce Points.

Photo advice: you can be sure of one thing, all those magnificent photos of Bryce displayed at the Visitor Center or in the gift shop at Ruby's Inn were taken either early in the morning or late in the afternoon. If you arrive at Bryce during the middle of the day and only stay a few hours, you can't hope to come away with professional quality photos.

Thor's Hammer and other shining hoodoos (Photo by Scott Walton)

The canyon's formations must have a warm light skimming their surface, whether from the back or the side, to bring out the relief and color. If you want to bring home high quality photos, you should be at one of the amphitheater viewpoints at dawn and use the rest of the morning to descend into the canyon. Watch out for overexposures which will wash out the ochers, yellows and oranges of the spires.

Time required: to get the most out of Bryce, it's advisable to stay at one of the motels in the area so you can visit the park in the early morning hours. It's also recommended that you take at least one hike on the canyon trails, an experience which involves a bit of effort.

Allow two and a half hours by car to visit the amphitheater viewpoints and one and a half hours to hike the canyon. If you don't have much time, go straight to Sunset Viewpoint. The Rim Trail running between Sunrise and Sunset Viewpoints and Inspiration Point is an easy walk if you don't want to descend into the canyon proper.

Early morning light on the Silent City

Inspiration Point and Bryce Point

Inspiration Point offers the best view of the extraordinary conglomeration of spires that make up the Silent City, situated in a recess to the south of Sunset Point. It's also possible to photograph the Silent City from Sunset Point. The Rim Trail between Sunset and Inspiration Point displays a constant stream of spectacular views. You can easily stroll it in about twenty minutes. You'll find the crowds much thinner at both Bryce and Inspiration Points, which could make your photography a lot easier in Summer.

Navajo and Queen's Garden Trails

To really absorb the magic of Bryce, a descent into the canyon is a must. Many trails run among the hoodoos and take you right into the middle of these formations. Two of these, Queen's Garden Trail (about a mile and a half) and Navajo Trail (about 2.2 miles) carry most of the foot traffic. This is due not only to their location in the amphitheater and their beauty, but because they are short and easy to reach. Both trails are interesting, though in the author's eyes, Navajo is more impressive. The Navajo descends from Sunset Point, passing by the famous rock chimney called Thor's Hammer and quickly arrives among the spires of Wall Street, which seem immense when viewed from below. The trek is short and not particularly difficult, except for the

Thor's Hammer (Photo by Steve Berlin)

ascent on the way back. The Queen's Garden Trail begins at Sunrise Viewpoint and is rather short. It's not as steep as the Navajo and it's more frequented as well. Each of these two trails will take about one to one and a half hours to complete. All the trails in the amphitheater are connected and you can make a loop using the Navajo and the Queen's Garden Trails in a little over two hours' time. By then you'll understand why old Ebenezer Bryce called this canyon "a hell of a place to lose a cow" as you take in the views, each more spectacular than the last.

Note: these two trails are about 8,000 feet in altitude. It can be extremely hot and dry in the summer and it is imperative you carry a canteen of water, a sun hat and sunscreen. You can hike these trails in jogging shoes without much problem but use extreme caution, especially on the steeper parts. These trails are often snow-covered starting in October and continuing until the end of April. Descent can be extremely risky without the right kind of boots. Once inside the canyon, though, snow and ice are less of a problem and the going is not so steep.

Fairyland Viewpoint and Trail

This viewpoint, as well as the trail of the same name, is frequently neglected by visitors who tend to congregate around the more famous ones near the amphitheater. Fairyland is just as lovely and gives you a completely different view of the canyon and its formations. This part of the canyon is more wooded and more touches of green are sprinkled against the red and orange rock chimneys. If you lack the time to do the Navajo or Queen's Garden Trail, try following the first 1,500 feet of the Fairyland Trail until you reach the promontory which you'll see a bit to the left of the viewpoint. The walk is easy and the view on both sides of the promontory is magnificent.

Yovimpai Point and Rainbow Point

These two viewpoints, at the southernmost tip of the park, appear very different from the amphitheater. You won't find similar scenery there. This is a superb alpine landscape and an interesting contrast after the amphitheater, if you have the time. The route climbs imperceptibly to the heart of a forest where pines and aspens blend. You'll find lots of wildlife here and an almost total absence of cars. From Yovimpai Point, the view takes in all the steps of the Grand Staircase to the south. From Rainbow Point, close to 8,500 feet in elevation, you have a sensational, unobstructed panorama of the Pink Cliffs, the highest tread on the Grand Staircase. It's also a good chance to view some ancient bristlecone pines and take spectacular photos of the tortuous forms of these members of the world's oldest living plant species. Some of their cousins in California's White Mountains are 6,000 years old and still growing.

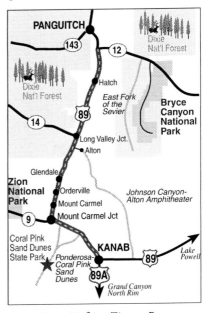

Route 89 from Zion to Bryce

AROUND BRYCE

Red Canyon

Red Canyon, under the jurisdiction of the Dixie National Forest, is an excellent prelude to Bryce if you are coming from Zion. For the majority of visitors, Red Canyon usually means a quick stop along the side of the road to snap a few shots before continuing on to Bryce. That's too bad since Red Canyon has a personality all its own. Its formations are definitely different from those of Bryce. For off-season visitors, arriving in greater numbers all the time, it's a first-rate alternative to the icy, snowbound trails of Bryce.

Red Canyon State Park

Two trails are available to you. The easiest and most pleasant is without doubt Pink Ledges, a loop of about twenty minutes, starting from the Visitor Center and passing several extremely esthetic viewpoints. The trail is very easy and a perfect alternative for those who don't want to tackle the Navajo or Queen's Garden Trails.

Much more difficult is the Birdseye Trail, located down from the Visitor Center. This trail climbs steeply to the heights and contains some superb vistas. The contrast between the abrupt halt of the angular formations and the peaceful valley of the Sevier below is interesting to observe.

The Cassidy Trail, upstream from the Visitor Center, offers the hiker in search of solitude a pleasant stroll far from the crowd in a lovely, steeply-banked canyon bordered with trees.

Getting there: either by Scenic Byway 12 from Bryce or by way of the splendid Scenic Byway 89 connecting Bryce to Panguitch following the course of the Sevier River.

Photo advice: in adapting to the angles of the sun, the light is as good in the morning as in the afternoon. If the sun is very strong, be careful not to underexpose the red rock with matrix-type meters. Conversely, take care not to overexpose the rock. A setting of a half stop on either side should be enough to assure a perfect exposure. The East side of the Pink Ledges Trail is highly recommended for photography.

Time required: about 20 min. to 1 hour depending on the amount of time you have.

Cedar Breaks National Monument

This National Monument resembles Bryce, though it presents some original formations. Cedar Breaks is laid out in the form of a vast, uninterrupted semi-circular amphitheater, deeper than Bryce and equally as colorful. Does it merit a detour? Without hesitation, yes, for enthusiasts desiring complete insight into the national parks of the Southwest, but no, for visitors who only have a week to ten days to do the Grand Circle.

Cedar Breaks' location is close to 10,000 feet high and the summit is often subjected to extremely violent winds. It closes early in autumn because of heavy snowfalls. The plateau is less obstructed than that of Bryce, with some good-size prairies interspersed among the forest pines. Route 14 between the valley of the Sevier River and Cedar City is absolutely lovely. In winter, the snow fields of Duck Creek are invaded by snowmobiles, a very tempting sight if you do not mind the noise.

Getting to Cedar Breaks

Getting there: from Scenic Byway 14 connecting Route 89 to Cedar City or from Scenic Byway 143 connecting Panguitch with Interstate 15. Coming from the north, you pass the ski resort at Brian Head.

Photo advice: four viewpoints allow you to photograph the amphitheater along the 5 mile long Scenic Drive; each one is a bit different from the other. If you are pressed for time, Point Supreme is probably the best, as well as the most crowded. The Wasatch Remparts trail is a nice walk with excellent late afternoon and evening views and allows you to photograph a rare group of very old Bristlecone pines at Spectra Point.

Time required: 1 h to 1 and 1/2 h to cross the park and take a few pictures from the viewpoints. Add a couple of hours for a leisurely stroll on the Wasatch Remparts trail.

Panorama from Bright Angel Point

Chapter 3
GRAND CANYON NATIONAL PARK

Bright Angel Point, Point Imperial and Cape Royal

It's understood that visiting the extraordinary geological phenomenon called the Grand Canyon is almost unavoidable. The Grand Canyon has become a must-see, a rite of passage in which one is obliged to participate in the course of a visit to the American West. Granted. But why not see the Grand Canyon from the North Rim? The north side of the Grand Canyon is truly a pleasure compared with the carnival-like atmosphere of the south side. Knowing the number of people who express their disappointment with the south side on their return from the Grand Canyon, the author doesn't hesitate recommending that you visit the North Rim and avoid the South Rim altogether. The route from Bright Angel Point to Cape Royal following the north bank of the Colorado River offers stupendous views of the canyon. It's probably true that the prettiest views to be had are on the south side but these scenes are photographed over and over. The sweeping vista from the North Rim is a bit more open, but equally satisfying to contemplate and you can come back with some original images.

This itinerary offers an additional advantage. Considering a fairly typical trip from Los Angeles or Las Vegas, it allows you to quickly reach Zion and Bryce and other areas along the northern side of the Colorado River before Page. You can get to the heart of the plateau faster and at the same time avoid the long, dull trip from L.A. to the Williams or Flagstaff roads on the south side of the river. You also save a precious day when coming back from Arches and Canyonlands, the end of the Grand Circle for most visitors. You can return by way of Capitol Reef and Bryce and visit or revisit many sites on the Colorado plateau.

Getting there: by Route 67 from Jacob Lake, midway between Kanab and Page on Route 89 Alt.

If you are traveling in mid-Fall or spring, you'll find the road closed even if there has been no snowfall. However, it's very easy to reach the canyon rim by taking the gravel road that parallels Route 67. A simple AAA map will help you find and follow it as it leaves Jacob Lake.

Photo advice: the views from the various vantage points around Bright Angel are fantastic in the late afternoon and should not be missed; a 35 mm lens will work very well there. For an unusual view of the canyon, don't miss Point Imperial, the highest point in the park offering a panoramic view of the Painted Desert with the magnificent spire of Mount Hayden in the foreground. Time permitting, drive down to Cape Royal for shots of Wotan's Throne and Vishnu's Temple.

Time required: a long half-day at the least from Jacob Lake.

Toroweap

For an exceptional view into the canyon, which is rectilinear in this spot with walls almost 3,000 feet high, Toroweap has no equal.

Getting there: from Route 89 Alt., you'll find the main road, called Mt. Trumbull Road, 7 miles west of Fredonia. This well-graded dirt/gravel road is passable year-round. You can come back by way of the trail leading to Colorado City. The latter is a clay road, which means it will be easier on your car—not mentioning your back—but it can become impassable for days on end after a serious rain. The dirt road to and from St. George is very scenic, but much longer, and it is often snowed-in during winter. The track deteriorates very badly past the Tuweep ranger station and the last two miles are quite difficult.

Photo advice: the view towards the east should be taken in late afternoon. Try using a person on one of the rock outcrops for added perspective. The view towards the west is more open and allows you to frame several miles of the Colorado River vertically.

Time required: unfortunately a very long half day is needed as you have 60 miles to go in each direction. This is one of the most isolated areas in the entire United States. Outside of the season and on a weekday, it is quite possible not to see anyone else on the road.

Toroweap looking East

Into the Canyon

The climb down into the canyon offers more in terms of personal satisfaction than photographic opportunities. If you have two days to devote, are in good physical condition, and have a good pair of hiking boots, you can have an unforgettable time. Here is a short description of the walk.

The recommended route is to descend by way of the South Kaibab Trail on the first day and ascend by the Bright Angel Trail on the second. The trail down is about 5 1/2 miles to Phantom Ranch and needs three or four hours to accomplish. The trail is extremely steep in parts. The temperature rises as you descend and it is imperative that you carry a good-size water container. This warning should be taken seriously. The author encountered a young Japanese hiker climbing up the South Kaibab Trail without water who was completely dehydrated and suffering from sunstroke. The first photographic opportunity occurs about a mile down the trail at a point where you can get a lovely panorama of the canyon. A lot of hikers don't go all the way to the bottom and you wouldn't be alone if you stopped here. On the other hand, there are fewer hikers below this point and you are free to experience the euphoria that surrounds such an experience. At about 4 miles, you come to a platform with a good, unimpeded view of the river and a suspension bridge leading to Phantom Ranch. At this point you are but a few feet

Yaki Point (Photo by Scott Walton)

above the Colorado River, that indefatigable architect of this majestic work at the base of which you now find yourself. It's an unforgettable experience.

The personnel at Phantom Ranch will get you up at 4:30 a.m. on the second day and after a hearty breakfast you'll be on the trail by 6:00 a.m. The Bright Angel Trail runs along the Colorado for about a mile before turning towards the plateau. (It would be more correct to say "the plateaus", plural, because the ascent is really a series of steps.) The trail is a little over 10 miles long with an elevation gain of more than 4,500 feet. The first part is marked by an absence of sun until you get to Indian Gardens where you can drink from the springs and rest in the shade before continuing to the summit. This second part is in sun and distinctly more difficult. The estimate by the National Park Service to complete the ascent is rather conservative. You should be able to finish it in six or seven hours at an easy pace.

If you don't have the time to make this long and extraordinary journey, but still wish to enter the canyon, the first viewpoint on the South Kaibab Trail is closer and more interesting than Indian Gardens on the Bright Angel Trail.

Getting there: it's possible to make the descent in one day if you are a cross-country runner. But for mere mortals, two days are necessary, which implies an overnight rest at Phantom Ranch either camping or staying in the dormitory (there are a few cabins for couples). Theoretically, reservations to stay at Phantom Ranch should be made way in advance, however, in reality there are a substantial number of cancellations. The best way to obtain a reservation is to call the main reservation line for the Grand Canyon National Park Lodges at (602) 638-2401 to inquire about availability. The day of the descent, leave your car in the parking lot of the El Tovar Hotel and take a shuttlebus or taxi to Yaki Point at the head of the South Kaibab trail. A morning departure is recommended to avoid the extreme heat of the day.

Photo advice: South Kaibab Trail offers the best views. In addition, it takes more time going down and up the Bright Angel Trail and so the South Kaibab is the best place to shoot the majority of your photos. You can reach a very lovely viewpoint after descending less than a mile, though you must go about three or four miles further down to get your

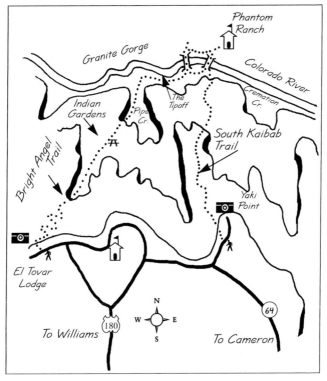

Descending into the Grand Canyon

first good glimpse of the Colorado River. Bright Angel Trail doesn't offer many quality photo opportunities outside of the first mile along the river. If you carry a small automatic camera it's sufficient and won't burden you with heavy equipment.

The White House ruins

Chapter 4
CANYON DE CHELLY

Before beginning, it should be said that this National Monument is pronounced "Canyon de Shay".

This superb canyon merits a detour, time permitting, and it really is a detour. Going to Canyon de Chelly, an entire day will evaporate as if by magic. If you decide to go, it's probably because your eye will have been irresistibly drawn to a superb shot of Spider Rock or again, to the famous scene of the Anasazi ruins of White House nestled beneath a striated, gilded wall of desert varnish. They're classics! The author himself once dreamed of one day visiting Canyon de Chelly after seeing it in the film "McKenna's Gold" in a theater in New Delhi.

If you visit Canyon de Chelly, concentrate on the south fork of the river which is definitely more interesting. The north fork of the river follows the Canyon del Muerto and really doesn't leave a memorable impression. It isn't possible to go down into the canyon without a Navajo guide, with the exception of the trail leading to the White House ruins. Curiously, this park is under the jurisdiction of the federal government, in contrast to Monument Valley, which is a Tribal Park administered by the Navajo Nation. However, it is inhabited by various Navajo families who graze their sheep and livestock in the bottom of the canyon. The author has never visited the canyon in the company of one of these Navajo guides, but no doubt it would be a really interesting experience.

The trail leading to White House zigzags for about a mile along the flank of the canyon, but is not very difficult. After a descent of about 400 feet you'll have to ford the river. It's not very deep and you'll get to the ruins soon. Out-of-season, the river is frozen. The walk to the ruins is superb and it would be a shame to miss. Besides, after all that driving a bit of a walk will come as a relief.

Getting there: by route 191, off of Interstate 40 south or from Mexican Water to the north. You can also take the 59 after Kayenta or the 264 at Tuba City. The landscape is pretty bleak and the lone Navajo pickup crossing your path will be the sole break in the monotony of the drive.

Photo advice: the highlight of any photographic trip to Canyon de Chelly is the classic view of the White House ruins, with their strings of desert varnish, from White House Overlook. There are a number of remarkable views offered from the edge of the canyon, but none equals the one of the monumental Spider Rock that rises into the sky like a gigantic antenna into the heavens. The best lighting is in the afternoon in summer and you'll need a very wide-angle lens to get it all in, though this isn't absolutely necessary. The ruins themselves make for excellent shots from the canyon floor. A medium telephoto will perfectly capture it all. The author has not been inside the canyon in the company of Navajo guides but has heard enthusiastic reports about it.

Time required: 1/2 day there, plus travel time. In the end, a whole day quickly evaporates with the long, boring drive to get there.

Desert varnish above the White House ruins

Kodachrome Basin at dusk

Chapter 5
GRAND STAIRCASE-ESCALANTE

Officially designated a National Monument by President Clinton in 1995, Grand Staircase-Escalante encompasses a vast region between Bryce Canyon and Capitol Reef. Crossing it from east to west is Scenic Byway 12. This route passes through some of the most grandiose scenery in Utah. The mountainous area around Boulder is absolutely spectacular and has magnificent views of Waterpocket Fold, the Henry Mountains and beautiful aspen forests offering great photographic opportunities year-round. The Henry Mountains are still a rarely visited wilderness and were not completely explored until the 1930's. Lack of funds and the need to accommodate the various and diverse needs of resident farmers, ranchers, miners, loggers and others, have kept the monument's administration in the hands of the B.L.M. The headquarters of the park are in Escalante, which is also the site of half a dozen motels, making it an excellent base for exploration.

Scenic Byway 12

This route is always spectacular no matter how you approach it. Photographically speaking, you get the best results from the viewpoints on Boulder Mountain in the afternoons. Crossing Boulder Mountain—an ancient volcano over 50 million years old—offers superb panoramas of Capitol Reef and the Henry Mountains from the viewpoints at Larb Hollow and Steep Creek. But the most beautiful viewpoint of all is the Homestead, where your eye embraces hundreds of miles around including the Waterpocket Fold, the Circle Cliffs, and the Burr Trail. Near the summit of SB12, you can photograph aspen forests. Fall colors are usually at their peak during the second week in October.

The Boyton Overlook—at the end of a ridge crest road with a shear drop on both sides—is mildly interesting and doesn't make for a good photograph. The 5.4 mile R/T walk to 125 feet tall LowerCalf Creek Falls is easy and rewarding. Although not in the same league as better known waterfalls, they make an interesting photograph. Avoid weekends, when the place is swarming with locals looking for a cool spot.

The view from Homestead Viewpoint

Anasazi State Park

Coming into Boulder, this State Park gives you brief glimpses of the environment and daily life of the original inhabitants—a group called the Basketmaker Pueblo—who settled this region. This area formed the northernmost extent of Anasazi influence just before their mysterious disappearance around 1300 A.D.

The museum was entirely refurbished in 1997 and has many interesting interactive exhibits. Behind the museum there is a replica of a typical Anasazi-type ancestral dwelling and a little further up the trail, the excavated ruins of the Coombs site.

Getting there: it's just outside Boulder to the north. Boulder is so tiny, it's hard to call it even a hamlet.

Photo advice: the reconstructed Anasazi dwelling and the pithouse make for interesting documentary-type photos.

Time required: 30 minutes to 1 hour.

The Burr Trail

The Burr Trail is an old track used by the Mormon pioneers when moving their livestock from the high-altitude pastures of Boulder Mountain to the warmer grazing areas of the Waterpocket Fold. The trail, graded and oiled in the 1980's, crosses magnificent country that is still wild and lonely, taking you to Capitol Reef.

Off the Burr Trail, narrows aficionados can visit Little Death Hollow. If you are one of them, get yourself a copy of the book by Michael Kelsey, Canyon Hiking Guide to the Colorado Plateau (see the Bibliography in the Appendix) or get directions from the B.L.M. rangers in Escalante who regularly visit the site. Be careful of spring and summer rainstorms as well as rain and snow during other seasons. The east end of the Burr Trail is covered in greater detail in the chapter on Capitol Reef.

Photo advice: about halfway between Boulder and Strike Valley, the road follows a narrow canyon; its walls are eroded in the form of highly concentrated deep holes dug into the rock; this phenomenon is known as Swiss Cheese and makes for interesting photography. Coming from Boulder, there is a nice panorama before you drop down into this canyon and again as you exit, when the view opens up on the Waterpocket Fold and the Henry Mountains.

Escalante Petrified Forest State Park

This is an interesting alternative to the better known—and more spectacular—Petrified Forest National Park. As the name indicates, this Utah state park was once an ancient forest engulfed millions of years ago by an inland sea. You'll find many multicolored petrified tree trunks. Because of its close proximity to Escalante, a quick visit is easy to include in your plans. The moderately difficult Wide Hollow Trail winds about a mile through juniper and pinyon pines before reaching the petrified trees and a viewpoint overlooking Escalante.

Getting there: located just south of Escalante next to the lovely Wide Hollow Reservoir. There is not much to see near the parking lot, so if you don't have an hour or don't care to walk, don't bother with this detour.

Photo advice: other than the large quantity of petrified trees, you'll find a forest of pygmy junipers and ancient dwarf pines that make for interesting photos, as well as a miniature version of the Painted Desert with lovely colors. The Sleeping Rainbow trail spur adds about 3/4 mile to your visit but it's a worthwhile detour to take for extreme close-ups of the petrified trunks.

Time required: 1 and 1/2 hours for a comfortable visit.

Kodachrome Basin State Park

This little Utah state park has some very interesting formations of Entrada sandstone, but it is the sand pipes—spectacular rock columns forming surreal fingers pointing to the sky—that give esthetic and geologic originality to the place. The columns are cut in a beige colored rock. Large Entrada sandstone monoliths take on a spectacular red at sunset superbly complementing this panorama. Campsites are available, but the park has become extremely popular in the last few years and you must make reservations for summer or holiday camping. Lots of easy trails ranging from a half mile to 3 miles will take you among the formations.

If time and your plans permit, make the detour to Kodachrome Basin around sunset, you won't regret it.

Getting there: from Scenic Byway 12, angle south to Cannonville exit (on your right coming from Bryce) and follow the signs for about 9 miles on the well-maintained Cottonwood Canyon Road, which is classified as a Scenic Backway.

Photo advice: leave the car in the parking lot or at the campsite and follow the trails. The main paved trail is marked with several information signs and takes only a dozen minutes to walk. It's full of interesting views

A sand pipe at Kodachrome Basin

of the finger-like formations mentioned above. For a better view of the park, follow the 1 mile long Grand Parade Trail, which passes by the more spectacular monoliths. The park is magnificent at sunset when the ocher sandstone walls become blood red and it certainly deserves its name.

Time required: from Route 12, 2 hours round trip with about 1 and 1/2 hours to tour the park.

Cottonwood Canyon Road

This is perhaps the most interesting Scenic Backway in Utah. This road is usually easily traveled by cars and motorhomes. You should nonetheless stop for information in Kanab, Page or Cannonville before embarking as heavy rains can make the road impassable. Signs will warn you not to take this route if rain is threatening. This is not an empty warning. After a heavy summer deluge, the route can become a muddy morass in just a few minutes and trap a vehicle with normal traction.

If conditions are favorable, which is most of the time, this route is truly enchanting. You'll want to make a number of stops along the way, easily stretching the hour it takes to drive it in a hurry into a much longer time. Whether you're coming from Bryce or from Escalante on your way to Page, don't count on using Cottonwood Road as a short-cut. It's possible to camp anywhere along the road since Escalante National Monument is administered by the B.L.M., and their policy concerning camping in the wild is very liberal.

Getting there: from Scenic Byway 12, angle south towards the Cannonville exit (on the right when coming from Bryce) and follow the signs of the Scenic Backway. After leaving Kodachrome Basin to your left, continue straight ahead. If you are coming from Route 89, you'll find the road about halfway between Page and Kanab; you'll need to pay close attention since there is only a small sign that is not clearly visible from the road.

Photo advice: there's magnificent scenery all along this route: a high plateau to the north, in the center a splendid valley of spectacular formations bordered by trees, and colorful "badlands" in the south. Many interesting spots border the Cottonwood Road from north to south. Round Valley Draw, an extremely photogenic slot canyon is unfortunately difficult to access unless you have a 4WD vehicle, a rope and a bit of experience in scaling and rappelling heights. That sort of adventure is outside the scope of this book. If you want to explore Round Valley Draw, get a copy of Michael Kelsey's excellent publication, <u>Canyon Hiking Guide to the Colorado Plateau</u> (see the Bibliography in the

Strange mound on Cottonwood Canyon

Appendix). The 4x4 track going to Round Valley Draw is marked by a sign about 7 miles south of Kodachrome Basin. Grosvenor Arch, a lovely double arch, is situated about a mile along a side route and is worth the detour. There is a sign marking the well-graded track. The Cottonwood Wash Narrows are only moderately spectacular but they have the advantage of being close to the road. You'll find them about 4 miles south of the intersection with the Grosvenor Arch trail where a bridge spans the wash.

If you can fit this magnificent track into your itinerary, you'll have an adventure that few visitors ever experience and memories that will be with you for a lifetime.

Time required: between 2 and 5 hours depending on how often you want to stop.

Hole-in-the-Rock Road

The Hole-in-the-Rock Road was constructed by Mormon pioneers after crossing the Colorado River and it was an incredible engineering feat to blast and cut through the rock flanks. Today, most of it is covered by the waters of Lake Powell, but a good part of the trail leading to the ford is still visible.

The two main stops on the trail are described in detail below and are easily accessible. To visit the actual spot called Hole-in-the-Rock, is an entirely different matter because the last 10 miles are quite difficult and require a 4x4 vehicle. Also, as the round trip is about 110 miles from Escalante you'd have to devote an entire day to it.

Escalante's Devil's Garden

Don't confuse this site with another of the same name located in the extreme northern section of Arches National Park. Here, they are referring to an extraordinarily spectacular group of petrified sand dunes, monoliths, arches and hoodoos. The Straight Cliffs form an interesting backdrop when photographing these formations.

Just outside the classic Grand Circle circuit, Devil's Garden is little visited but warrants a detour because of its proximity to Escalante and the considerable photographic potential it offers. If you are spending the night in Escalante, it's possible to make a quick visit at sunrise or sunset.

There isn't any marked trail and you can wander as you please in the Devil's Garden. However, your natural tendency will be to make a loop around these curiosities following the traces of previous visitors to the top. The spectacular petrified dunes are among the most beautiful on the Colorado Plateau and are to be found at the highest part of the site, about 1,500 feet from the parking lot.

Getting there: located along the Scenic Backway leading to Hole-in-the-Rock, just 12 miles from where it branches off Scenic Byway 12. The gravel-covered road is well maintained for the first 50 miles, beginning 6 miles to the east of Escalante on Scenic Byway 12. Except during or immediately after a violent storm, it should not present any difficulties for the ordinary passenger car until you get to Devil's Garden or Coyote Gulch. Nevertheless, it's advisable to stop at the B.L.M. ranger station in Escalante before going, to check conditions.

Photo advice: morning light or early evening is always preferred with this type of spectacular formation, but the terrain and the angles vary so it's possible to get some good shots even in the middle of the day. However, the prettiest photos are taken in the morning when the Straight Cliffs are well lit in the background. Generally the best angles are almost all found facing these Straight Cliffs.

Metate Arch

Time required: 2 hours round trip from Escalante for a brief visit, but you could easily spend 2 or 3 hours taking photos here. If combining this visit with Coyote Gulch and Peek-a-Boo, you'll need about 6 hours.

The Slot Canyons of Coyote Gulch

Located about 30 miles outside Escalante, Coyote Gulch is a unique opportunity to explore several spectacular slot canyons without crowds and commercial trappings. Take advantage of it now as that's bound to change. Coyote Gulch combines several canyons.

The narrows proper are located immediately to the left of the dry river bed. Though not in the same league as the more famous narrows of the Virgin River or those of Buckskin Gulch, they are nonetheless quite spectacular. The walls, a lovely ocher color of Navajo sandstone, are about 10 to 15 feet apart and around 70 feet high. A few minutes walking in the narrows gives those who don't want to venture into the slot canyons a chance to shoot some nice pictures.

Peek-a-boo is an absolute must for slot canyon devotees. It's an extremely narrow and twisted passage about half a mile long, blessed with excellent lighting due to the low height of its Navajo sandstone walls. You can find it easily at the bottom of the trail from the parking lot near the junction of the narrows and the dry creek bed of Coyote Gulch. Peek-a-boo is in the form of a fault in the wall of Coyote Gulch. You can only get into it by climbing up the wall, but toeholds cut in the rock will help and no special equipment is needed. Once you've overcome this part, getting into the narrow passage of Peek-a-boo, your progress will be easier. However, you must not be claustrophobic. You'll have to wriggle through a narrow rock tunnel located about 150 feet from the entrance to be able to explore the upper part of the canyon, where you can only advance one step at a time scraping the bottom of your pants. The most spectacular twists and turns are found barely 600 feet from the entrance of the canyon. With the arrival of more and more visitors since the creation of the National Monument, this extraordinary canyon risks becoming a popular destination for lovers of the

The entrance to Peek-a-Boo Canyon

bizarre. The canyon supposedly harbors a dwarf species of rattlesnake. Fortunately it's not supposed to be aggressive, but you need to be careful where you step.

Spooky is the next slot canyon down Coyote Gulch to the southeast. It's incredibly narrow and, as its name indicates, spooky. You can easily enter it from the riverbed of Coyote Gulch and a few steps are enough to give you a good idea of its appearance. To explore it completely would require special equipment and is outside the scope of this guide. Spooky presents little interest to the photographer, the walls being very close together and not particularly photogenic. Light, when there is any, is extremely limited.

Getting there: to reach Coyote Gulch, follow the Hole-in-the-Rock Scenic Backway 14.5 miles past Devil's Garden (this is 26.5 miles from the fork with Route 12). Then follow a very rough, but nevertheless passable, track for a mile and a half to the parking lot. This track is easily located by the presence of a solitary juniper on the right side. Be sure to bear left at the spot where the track forks. Leaving the parking lot, a trail about half a mile long descends to the dry riverbed of Coyote Gulch. The trail is marked by rock cairns, but it's not easy to follow. Keep your eyes constantly on the cairns.

Photo advice: a wide angle is indispensable in these narrow slot canyons to capture as much as possible of the rock walls on film, as well as to maximize the depth-of-field and avoid blurring the rock walls in the foreground. A tripod is necessary to work with an opening of f/16 or f/22 with slow slide film. With 50 or 100 ISO film, which is typical of slide film, you will find yourself exposing for half a second to several seconds depending on the sunlight. Peek-a-boo's good overall lighting makes it possible to work with a hand-held camera, using ISO 400 or 800 negative film, but you'll pay the price in lack of depth-of-field. It would be ideal to have one camera body for photos taken with slow shutter speeds on a tripod and another for those candid shots of people that these narrow canyons allow you to shoot. It's useless to carry several lenses as there's a good chance of scraping them against the walls. If you are taking stock photographs, pay close attention to small details. In the excitement of the moment, it's easy to forget the messy footprints in the foreground, to give but one example.

Time required: 4 hours round-trip from Escalante if you don't dawdle and visit Devil's Garden at the same time; 6 hours round-trip for a more leisurely trip to both.

Crawling deep inside Peek-a-Boo

Scenic Byway 12 from Bryce to Capitol Reef

Giant monoliths in Upper Cathedral Valley

Chapter 6
CAPITOL REEF NATIONAL PARK

This extraordinary park is often overlooked by visitors to the Land of the Canyons and isn't heavily frequented—2,500 people a day at the height of summer. This is certainly due to its geographic location, which makes it less accessible than its neighbors Bryce and Arches, but perhaps also to the fact that would-be visitors find it difficult to visualize its many sights. Nevertheless, Capitol Reef is one of the best guarded secrets of Utah. But be forewarned! This park doesn't reveal itself easily to the casual visitor. Sure, you can cross it in a few hours, even include the famous Scenic Drive, but it's off the beaten track where you'll find the best scenery.

One of the principal attractions of Capitol Reef is the great geological diversity of its sedimentary layers. This translates into an extraordinary palette of hues and textures, great for visitor and photographer alike. You can better appreciate this extraordinary relief with a bit of knowledge, however superficial, of the paleoenvironment of Capitol Reef, its sedimentary layers, and the forces of erosion that are constantly at work exposing them. Free brochures are available for travelers at the Visitor Center. Don't miss this opportunity as Capitol Reef, more than any other park, gives you a tremendous insight into the geologic history of the Land of the Canyons—the essential ingredient behind these landscapes that we so much admire today.

Either of two small towns can serve as a base for your exploration:

Torrey, at the west entrance or Hanksville at the east. Over the course of the last few years, these have both seen a great deal of expansion. In the 1980's there wasn't a single motel in either Torrey or Hanksville and now there are a dozen in each. Camping at Fruita is especially nice if you are car camping or want to pitch a tent.

Panorama Point & the Goosenecks of the Sulphur

It's strongly recommended that you make a quick detour to Panorama Point, a promontory where you can obtain a splendid panoramic view of the western section of the park with Capitol Dome, the Castle and the Henry Mountains in the distance. A National Park Service sign claims that this spot is the least polluted in the United States and that on a clear day you can see over a hundred and thirty miles! Even though the validity of this claim is doubtful today, you'll certainly rejoice in the fact that you can see a at least 60 miles on any given day.

It's also an excellent view to the west in the direction of Torrey. You can use a normal lens and mornings are usually best. Toward the east, a 100 to 200 mm telephoto lens works great for capturing Capitol Dome and the Henry Mountains in the afternoon.

The Goosenecks of Sulphur Creek are not particularly awe-inspiring, but it's a quick trip. A mile down the dirt road, you'll find a short, 1/3 mile trail leading to a promontory above a deep canyon that is strongly shadowed and difficult to photograph. Nothing to compare with the "big guys" (Dead Horse Point, Horseshoe Bend, and Goosenecks State Park), but it's interesting to note that these goosenecks are cut through the same layer of sedimentary rock as that of the White Rim of Island in the Sky fame, a formation only rarely seen on the plateau.

The Castle towers over Fruita

Fruita

This old Mormon colony is located on the banks of the Fremont River and has abundant vegetation, contrasting heavily with the surrounding desert. Several cabins containing pioneer-era artifacts are visible from the road and warrant a brief stop.

Autumn morning on the Fremont River

The cottonwoods bordering the Fremont around Fruita are magnificent in spring and fall. The vast grassy area adjoining the picnic grounds with its peaches, wisterias and jacarandas allows you to get some great shots when they're in flower (March and April). Following Route 24 in the direction of Hanksville, the Fremont presents a festival of colors with a number of orchards in which you are allowed to pick the fruit. The countless tamarisk trees lining the riverbed are particularly photogenic in autumn.

Sulphur Creek, which empties into the Fremont River beside the campground at Fruita, is a particularly lovely walk. Just behind the Visitor Center, a short footpath quickly brings you to a series of lovely pools.

In all seasons, Fruita is an oasis where it's nice to relax between two rocky landscapes.

Chimney Rock and the Castle

Chimney Rock is somewhat lacking in interest and makes you wish there was more to it. From the parking lot, Chimney Rock can't be photographed with a good light until the afternoon. By then, the dark red of the Moenkopi formation capped by the white Shinarump sandstone is really spectacular.

As for the Castle, it offers a remarkable collection of sedimentary layers that can be enjoyed right by the side of the road and photographed all day long.

The Scenic Drive

The Scenic Drive, which begins a bit after you pass Fruita, offers some spectacular views of domes all along a well-maintained dirt road.

Grand Wash and Capitol Gorge are worth the trip, though they don't give the same impression of isolation and adventure as some of the narrower and less visited canyons described in this book. Get yourself one of the mini-guides to the Scenic Drive at the entrance and stop at the various landmarks, following the interesting explanations it contains on the sedimentary origins of the park.

The Scenic Drive is superb in the morning returning from Capitol Gorge, but it's in the afternoon that you can get the best light on the sensuous, light-colored Navajo sandstone walls of Capitol Ridge.

The Scenic Drive near Grand Wash

Introduction to Cathedral Valley

Cathedral Valley is, in the eyes of the author, one of the most remarkable spots on the planet. An incomparable majesty emanates from the place. Its remoteness and the rare presence of other members of our species make you feel deeply privileged to find yourself in such an untrammeled natural sanctuary.

Happily or unhappily, it is not easy to visit and most visitors to the park abstain from venturing there.

Getting there: there is a 60-mile loop crossing many distinctive parts of the valley. This road is only feasible if you have a high clearance vehicle. It is not advised to drive this road in a regular car—even though

Cathedral Valley monolith in the evening light

the author has seen it done on rare occasions—and even less so in a camper. It all depends on the state of the road at the particular time. This can vary a lot, depending on whether you are traveling before or after rains or when the bulldozer resurfaces the road, once a year.

Instead of doing the whole loop, it's possible to reach several parts of the valley from various side roads. The main attractions of the valley are described separately below.

The following recommendations concerning driving apply to all of these sites:

Never set out until you have first inquired of one of the local residents as to the condition of the road. The local farmers often have a better appreciation of the difficulties than the rangers who systematically discourage visitors from adventuring down these roads in ordinary cars. They do this with good reason. Each year visitors get stuck in the mud or a rut that suddenly appeared from nowhere. As a general rule, a 4x4 towing-truck costs $150 an hour from the time it leaves the garage. The cost of the operation can easily reach $1,500 to $2,000 to bail you out. (The author knows of a case in Death Valley where towing cost the owner of a 4x4 vehicle $2,500 because, panicked by the state of the road, he tried to turn around. The loose dirt collapsed under his rear wheels and he went over the edge, flipping upside down and landing with his tires in the air.) The Cathedral Valley road is a perfect example of a "feasible" road, that's nevertheless risky because of its fragility and isolation.

You really need to get a topographic map before setting out on any of the roads described below. All these roads include many branching secondary roads that don't show on the large scale maps and it's easy to set off down the wrong path. This is not really a problem as you'll normally detect it quickly, but you could lose a lot of precious time if you're not paying attention. Please take this suggestion seriously. You'll often find yourself consulting your topo map. You can get one of these at the Visitor Center in Fruita.

Time required: 5 to 7 hours minimum for the loop. See individual times for each of the sites on the loop.

Colorful badlands and volcanic rock are found throughout Capitol Reef

The South Desert and the Bentonite Hills

The road overhanging the South Desert and the Bentonite Hills follows a dry riverbed between the extreme northern end of the Waterpocket Fold and the depression of Cathedral Valley. The Bentonite Hills are remarkable for their rounded forms and strange, checkerboard appearance colored by the Morrison formation. All the colors of the rainbow can be seen. Many exceptional viewpoints border the road as you follow it to the northwest from River Ford.

Lower South Desert Overlook encompasses a splendid view of Jailhouse Rock, with Temple Rock and the Fishlake Mountains in the background.

About 4 miles from the intersection with Lower South Desert Overlook, a one mile trail takes you to a view of Lower Cathedral Valley. If you think this view is splendid, wait until you're in the valley proper.

Further along the trail, Upper South Desert Overlook is very impressive and gives a good idea of the depth of the South Desert depression if you include a bit of the plateau in the foreground. Those suffering from fear of heights will certainly get weak in the knees.

Getting there: take the road from the so-called River Ford, located a dozen miles from the Visitor Center. The biggest problem will be the Fremont River crossing just a couple of hundred yards past the beginning of the track. The gate is locked after heavy rains and the Visitor Center rangers will let you know if it's passable or not. Beyond River Ford, the track is passable in a passenger car if you pay close attention and drive slowly and it's generally possible to make it to Lower South Desert Overlook. It's hard to say if you would get any further in an ordinary vehicle. It all depends on whether the bulldozer has been through recently.

Time required: 2 to 3 hours.

Upper Cathedral Valley

Located at the far north end of both the park and the Middle Desert, Upper Cathedral Valley is one of the highlights of Utah. The majesty that emanates from the powerful monoliths and the encircling mountains is reinforced by the isolation and effort it takes to get here.

The uppermost giant monolith at Upper Cathedral Valley

Once you're in the valley, there's a shallow footpath, marked by a sign saying "Viewpoint", to the right of the road coming from Cathedral Valley junction. It takes you up onto the plateau where you can get a spectacular view of the two main groups of monoliths with the Walls of Jericho in the background. A primitive campground with only six sites is located a bit higher close to the junction of two trails, one coming from the mountain and the other from River Ford. If you've come equipped, camping here will allow you to catch some fabulous evening shots of the extraordinary walls of Entrada sandstone as they turn bright red against a background of dark-gray sky. The Land of the Canyons at its very best!

Leaving the campground to your right and continuing up the switchbacks toward the plateau, you'll soon reach a junction with the Thousand Lakes road coming from the mountains and the one coming from South Desert. Follow the latter for about a mile until you come to Upper Cathedral Valley Viewpoint, from where you can admire Cathedral Valley in all its splendor. Another mile and you're at the Upper South Desert Overlook (see the South Desert above).

Near Upper Cathedral Valley, Gypsum Sinkhole—a gigantic, sunken artesian well almost 200 feet deep and over 50 feet in diameter—is well worth the mile-long detour on a good trail, though it's almost impossible to photograph because of its size.

Getting there: the easiest way for passenger cars and small size campers to get to this distant spot is from the north, by way of a dirt road leaving from the junction of Interstate 70 and Route 10, about 2 miles east of the town of Fremont Junction. This wide dirt road is well-maintained for the use of local miners and ranchers, and won't present any difficulties. The sole obstacle is crossing Willow Springs Wash, about a dozen miles down the road. After crossing the usually dry ford, the road quickly rolls along and you rapidly reach Upper Cathedral Valley.

It's also possible to reach it by following the South Desert track (see above) or the Lower Cathedral Valley track (see below). The most scenic—and difficult—access is by way of Route 72 coming from Loa, then taking the road to the right (about 7 miles down the 72). This track leads to the Elkhorn campground. The road is in excellent condition until you reach a high altitude pass (at about 10,000 feet) in the Fishlake National Forest. At the first fork in the road, continue straight ahead, following the signpost indicating Cathedral Valley. Here the descent becomes quite tricky and it is out of the question to take an ordinary passenger car over this portion of the road. A high-clearance 2WD vehicle might be able to make it, except in winter. This route is especially remarkable as it makes a spectacular transition between two radically different ecosystems, one a high-altitude alpine environment and the other the exceptional desert of Cathedral Valley. These mountains are the habitat of a great variety of wild animals—in the course of one trip, the author counted almost a hundred mule deer coming down the side of the mountain in great leaps and bounds.

Time required: you can reach Upper Cathedral Valley in approximately 1 hour from the Interstate offramp, provided you don't stray off the path. You'll definitely need a topo map. Count on 2 to 3 hours for any of the other routes. Getting there is one thing, but it's a shame if you can't devote at least a couple of hours to exploring this exceptional spot.

Lower Cathedral Valley

Lower Cathedral Valley is better known by the name of the two fantastic monoliths that it harbors. The Temple of the Sun and the Temple of the Moon illustrate many coffee-table books and well-deserve their names. Reaching up from the desert ground as if trying to grasp the heavens, these two solitary temples cut an imposing profile against a rich blue sky of unmatched purity. (Capitol Reef is said to be the least polluted spot in the United States.) At sunrise and sunset, these "high priests" of the mineral universe don their incandescent garments for a brief, fleeting moment, to celebrate the miracle of nature.

Getting there: to get to Lower Cathedral Valley and the famous Temples of the Sun and the Moon, it's best to come from Upper Cathedral Valley by way of the northern road described above, even if it means a much longer trip than via the Caineville Wash route described below. You'll nevertheless pass numerous washes between the two valleys

The Temple of the Moon at dawn

about a dozen miles apart and the state of the road can be extremely variable.

You can also get to Lower Cathedral Valley by following the Caineville Wash road (see the Caineville Badlands below).

Time Required: 2-4 hours round trip, just to get there, 1-3 hours once you're there.

The Waterpocket Fold

This strange and spectacular geologic formation is unfortunately less spectacular when seen from the ground than in the superb aerial photograph that decorates the National Park Service brochure. But it still warrants a detour if you can afford the whole day it will take.

You can get to the Waterpocket Fold by way of the Notom-Bullfrog road, which is paved along the first 6 miles and well-maintained thereafter. You get a very good view of the Henry Mountains to the east and the strange nipples of Capitol Dome to the west from the top of the hill, just after you reach the unpaved part of the road.

After rejoining the Burr Trail, a Scenic Backway to the south of the park, the road climbs to the Escalante Plateau in a series of spectacular twists and turns carved in the flank of the hill. This part of the road, about 5 miles long, is not surfaced but doesn't pose any problems for an ordinary car.

Getting there: it's possible to make a loop by descending the length of the Waterpocket Fold on the excellent Notom-Bullfrog road that you can take off of Route 24 where you see the sign for Notom. You can go back up by way of the Burr Trail—oiled in the eighties after much controversy—and proceed toward Boulder.

Following the Waterpocket Fold road all the way leads to the Bullfrog Marina, where you can cross Lake Powell by ferry to Hall's Crossing and either descend towards Monument Valley or climb back up towards Moab.

The Notom-Bullfrog Road meanders through badlands

Waterpocket Fold from Strike Valley Overlook

The route is usually passable in all seasons, but there is a wash before Sandy Ranch that can present problems in heavy rains or when it's icy in winter.

To go south on the ferry, consult the Glen Canyon chapter.

Photo advice: be forewarned that the Waterpocket Fold doesn't really become visible until after you pass the trail leading to the Cedar Mesa campground. Even there, this extraordinary geological phenomenon remains a bit disappointing seen from the Notom-Bullfrog road as compared with aerial photos. Only from Strike Valley Overlook or Upper Muley Twist will you be able to get some photos capturing the true expanse of the fold.

Time required: 4 to 5 hours for the drive from Fruita to Boulder via the Notom-Bullfrog road, with brief stops.

Strike Valley and Muley Twist

Strike Valley Overlook is a remarkable vista point, from where you can photograph the wide expanse of the Waterpocket Fold. It is a must if you are entering or exiting Capitol Reef from the Burr trail.

Getting there: via the Burr Trail from Boulder, via the Notom Bull-frog Road from either Fruita or Bullfrog. If you have a 4WD or high clearance vehicle, you can drive the 3 miles from the intersection with the Burr trail to the trailhead. It is a very rough road, but it is quite scenic and not dangerous. It's actually a good place to hone your boulder straddling skills if you are not an experienced four-wheeler. Do not attempt this road with a low clearance vehicle, you would become high-centered or would damage your undercarriage. Following the road on foot makes for a very pleasant hike, although you would not want to do this hike in Summer. Strike Valley Lookout is approximately half a mile from the trailhead parking and offers a fantastic panoramic view on the Waterpocket Fold.

If you decide to explore Upper Muley Twist, just follow the wash at the trailhead until you reach Saddle Arch, on your left, at a little under two miles. This Arch is not easy to spot at first, but the N.P.S. has recently added a small sign to the right of the wash indicating the Rim trail. It is a very rough climb up but you'll reach the top in less than 30 minutes and the rim of the plateau in another 10 minutes on flat ground. From there, the trail follows the rim North for another two miles, offering spectacular views of the Waterpocket Fold.

You can either retrace your steps or do the full loop coming back through the Upper Muley Twist Narrows, which are not particularly spectacular. Caution: Upper Muley Twist gets awfully hot in summer. Take plenty of water if you want to do the full loop.

Getting to Capitol Reef

Photo advice: from the Strike Valley trailhead, follow the rim to your right to the very end of the trail for the best photographic location; you'll find a rock outcrop that makes a good foreground to add depth to this otherwise huge panorama. Use your wide angle in moderation, otherwise you'll end up with an image that doesn't carry enough visual impact. A 35mm will work well, allowing you to include enough of the valley while emphasizing the gentle curve made by the Waterpocket Fold to the South.

Upper Muley Twist offers a very rewarding, albeit strenuous, hike and yields even more open panoramic views of the Waterpocket Fold. The views are a little more open than at Strike Valley, especially to the North, but are also harder to photograph successfully.

Time required: 2 to 3 hours by car, a half-day on foot; a full day for Upper Muley Twist.

The Caineville Badlands

The Caineville Badlands and Factory Butte

The Caineville Badlands are a vast isolated expanse of dark gray hills of Mancos shale striped with interesting colors. Traveling through the heart of these badlands, you'll encounter from time to time round blocks of basalt tossed out by the explosion of Boulder Mountain (see the chapter on the Grand Staircase/Escalante) about 50 million years ago and then later deposited here by glacial action. These badlands are actually very deep, forming a bed of sedimentary rock between 2,000 to almost 3,000 feet thick. While contemplating this extreme desert universe, it's easy to imagine the inland sea that once covered this part of the valley.

Taking in the view to the northeast, you'll see the imposing presence of Factory Butte rising on the horizon like a tall ship. This mesa consists of packed layers of Mancos shale.

Getting there: from Route 24, to the east of Capitol Reef, the road begins 8 miles east of River Ford, just before the place called Caineville. A sign by the side of the road indicates the distance to Lower and Upper Cathedral Valley. This road will take you right into a fantastic universe of badlands in just 2 or 3 miles. If you want to continue on to Cathedral Valley, this road can probably be negotiated with a passenger car, if the weather conditions are right, but it's a long drive and you'll be bounced and jolted the whole way.

Time required: 45 min. for a quick excursion into the heart of the badlands; 2 hours round trip for the drive alone if you continue on until Lower Cathedral Valley.

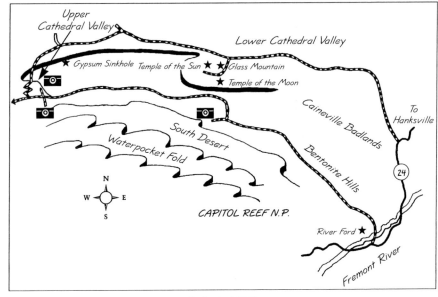

Cathedral Valley

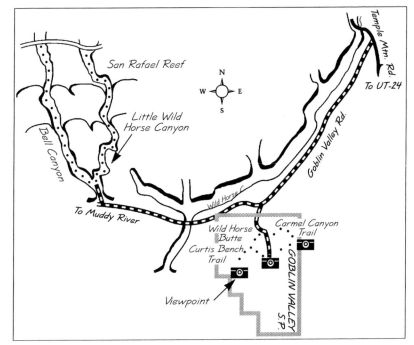

Goblin Valley & Little Wild Horse Canyon

Goblin Valley State Park

Chapter 7

THE SAN RAFAEL REEF

The San Rafael Reef is the southernmost part of the San Rafael Swell, an imposing circular plateau located west of the Green River on either side of Interstate 70. The Reef takes its name from its shape, that of a serrated reef, dominating this wild desert region. This reef consists of several sedimentary layers pushed almost vertically into position by the shifting of tectonic plates.

The author describes here two easy and highly photogenic trips that will leave you with lasting memories and some astounding photos.

Goblin Valley State Park

In Goblin Valley, erosion has carved an extremely pliable variety of Entrada sandstone into extravagant shapes offering your astonished eyes a spectacle of goblins, ghosts and other fantastic creatures seemingly awaiting a magic wand to awaken them and start them walking as if in an animated motion picture.

Many of these goblin formations line the road on the left, just before the entrance to the park, and deserve a photo if the light is right. But it's at the covered viewpoint at road's end that the most compelling sight awaits you—a vast army of goblins, camped in the depression below the parking lot, mineral creatures looking like something out of a Tolkien story. You can imagine them regrouping in secret for some imaginary assault on the planet.

Start your visit just by enjoying and photographing this panorama right from the observation point, as it is truly superb. In summer, you risk catching in your viewfinder lots of Lilliputian-sized humans photographing these ferocious goblins. This formerly little-known park now receives about 80,000 visitors a summer. Out of season, you'll have it all to yourself.

Goblin Valley has two official foot trails: the mile-long Carmel Canyon loop and the slightly longer Curtis Bench trail. The latter offers a superb view of the Henry Mountains from its highest point.

However, the most interesting walks simply consist of descending into the depression from the covered viewpoint and walking among the goblins where you can let your imagination run wild.

Getting there: you can reach this Utah State Park by Route 24 from Green River to the north or from Capital Reef to the south.

The cutoff from Route 24 is located 24 miles south of the intersection with Interstate 70 and 22 miles north of Hanksville. The first 7

miles of the road, classified as a Scenic Backway, are paved and the rest is a wide gravel road in excellent condition. Herds of antelope are frequently visible along the road. There is a 4x4 track south of the main road. This track heads straight for the park, but it's not suitable for passenger cars, or even a 4WD, after a rain which can wash out the road until the next time a bulldozer fixes it, sometimes months later.

Photo advice: there's a particularly remarkable spot that you just must go photograph. Crossing the basin at 1

Goblin generals preparing to attack

o'clock in the direction of the cliffs, look for a large copper green dome. It may look quite far from the observation point, but it's really only a short 10 minute walk. Climbing up, you'll find a passage leading behind a group of very high formations. You'll come out into a veritable fantasy land of spires and chimneys. It's possible to go even further for closer shots of the spires. It's a spot you shouldn't miss.

As with many other places, avoid visiting Goblin Valley when the sun is high in the sky as your pictures will have too much contrast and will look flat under a uniform sky. Ideally, early morning or evening is best as the main view of the depression is oriented to the south.

A strangely phallic mushroom rock

Little Wild Horse Slot Canyon

This highly rewarding mini-adventure, both very visual and tactile, lets you penetrate right into the heart of the San Rafael Reef. You're guaranteed to bring back some amazing shots from this trip inside Little Wild Horse Canyon.

Access is very easy and the walk through the canyon is not particularly difficult, except for the entrance, as we'll see.

After parking your car—having carefully read the instructions in Getting there—find the trail leading to the dry wash bed and follow it for a few hundred yards. As the riverbed narrows, you'll come to a sort of dry waterfall about 8 feet high that you'll have to climb. The best way to get around this obstacle is on the right following the narrow, inclined plane offering about 15 inches of toehold. This isn't really complicated, but watch out that you don't slip or hit your head on the rock above.

Follow along for about 200 yards after the dry fall and then turn right at the fork into Little Wild Horse Canyon. The other fork leads to Bell Canyon, which is not explored in this guide.

Little Wild Horse Canyon starts revealing its strange splendor a few hundred feet further on. It begins with a series of very interesting niches as well as ground and polished protrusions carved out by water action on the walls. At a height of about 200 feet, the latter are tightly constricted in some places and no more than a couple of feet wide at shoulder height. In some places, you'll need to place both hands on the rock wall and perform a series of push-up motions so you can move forward inside the highly slanted, shallow corridor. But, generally speaking, the walk is never very difficult. However, be careful you don't get stuck and twist an ankle when the fault contracts down to a few inches under your feet.

A narrow spot in the canyon

Follow your exploration up-canyon for as long as your heart desires but go at least a half mile to really take in the atmosphere of the place. After the first hundred yards or so, the slot canyon widens, but a second section, even narrower than the first, and also much more interesting, awaits you a bit further on. Keep walking until you reach a sort of bent amphitheater. The canyon continues on even higher, but by now you have done the most interesting part.

Getting there: leaving Goblin Valley State Park, turn left one mile further on a road marked by a sign saying Little Wild Horse Canyon. This road is generally well maintained and easily traveled in an ordinary passenger car or camper. Always get the latest information from the Goblin Valley rangers since you'll be crossing a very sandy wash about 3 miles from the intersection with the Goblin Valley road. In case of recent rains, the road may be washed out. You'll come to a parking lot in about 5 miles. In case of flash flooding, your car will be protected here as it is above the riverbed. A sign tells about such a flash flood experienced by a visiting couple, with a photo showing their Landcruiser washed away by the high water. Take this very seriously, particularly on a summer's afternoon. Flash floods are generated by rain falling on the Reef far above the entrance of the canyon and you won't necessarily see it. It can be perfectly dry when you get out of your car and be raining just a few miles away. If you are caught by a flash flood while you are in the canyon, you'll be in great danger. Never forget that it's storms such as these that are responsible for the creation of the magnificent walls of this slot canyon.

Photo advice: read the general recommendations on photography in the Introduction, as well as those specific to Peek-a-boo Canyon in the Grand Staircase/Escalante chapter. Little Wild Horse Canyon consists of a very brown type of Wingate and Kayenta sandstone on the ground with light colored Navajo sandstone on the very high walls. All this combines to make it quite dark.

Time required: 3 hours R/T, hike included, from Goblin Valley.

Polished rock protruding from a wall of Little Wild Horse Canyon
Turn the book over and watch the rock turn into holes.

The Colorado at Horseshoe Bend (Photo by Scott Walton)

Chapter 8
AROUND PAGE

Upper Antelope Canyon

Page has become a must-see destination on the route to the canyons since the discovery of Antelope Canyon by the media. Until the end of the 1980's, few people had heard of this extraordinary slot canyon and only a few stray professional photographers had ventured there.

In the old days, getting there was like playing roulette. If the Begays—the Navajo family responsible for the land of the Upper Antelope Canyon—weren't answering their phone or were unable to meet you at the gate, you were stuck.

At the time of the his first visit in the 1980's, the author had the luck to find one of the Begays to open the gate and was able to go on about his way quite happily in his own 4x4 vehicle. On his second visit, things were already a bit more organized and the LeChee Chapter of the Navajo Nation had taken over control of visits to Antelope Canyon. During the season, a guard was stationed at the gate in his truck and would open it for you after collecting $5. If you had a 4x4 vehicle, they'd leave you to go it alone. During the off-season, it was necessary to call ahead. The author spent a rainy afternoon in November calling the Begay children numerous times to ask that someone be sent to open the gate. After several round trips between Page and Antelope, and 3 or 4 hours lost, he gave up.

These bittersweet recollections will serve to illustrate how things have changed. Today, several accredited companies will take visitors in groups for a fee between $25 and $50, depending on whether the tour is qualified as "regular" or "for serious photographers".

In season, it's still possible to visit Upper Antelope Canyon without a guide by presenting yourself at the gate and paying $15 (or only $5 if you wish to leave your car and walk the 6 miles round trip on foot). Out of season, you'll have to go to the office of Navajo Parks and Recreation in Page (see Resources in the Appendix). At worst, you'll have to wait and go with a tour company the next day. If the weather is threatening rain, the visit will be canceled.

Getting there: leave Page by Route 98 going to Kaibito, aiming towards the power plant. The entrance to the canyon is two miles down this road on the right and is well marked. If you decide to go with an organized tour, consult the chapter on Resources in the Appendix.

Photo advice: Upper Antelope Canyon is at once both simple and difficult to photograph. Speaking of equipment, to obtain the best results, you'll really need a tripod. If you don't have one, you can rent one in town. A cable release is also recommended. If you don't have one, the self-timer on your camera will work just as well to prevent blurred pictures due to camera shake. Don't use a flash if you want to preserve the texture of the walls and the nuances of color created by natural light. However, the flash will give acceptable results if you are just taking shots of the family or trying to capture the general atmosphere of the canyon.

The Corkscrew

A ray of light filters through the Corkscrew (Photo by Steve Berlin)

The best time to visit the canyon is between 10 a.m. and 2 p.m., when the sun is at its zenith. This is a blessing for photographers, who rarely have such interesting possibilities during the middle of the day. Basically, the walls of the canyon are around 120 feet high and the sinuous nature of the narrow passage makes it difficult for the light to penetrate. Don't be put off by the absence of sunshine, take longer exposures and you'll be pleasantly surprised with the results. Also, consult the general photo advice for slot canyons in the Introduction.

Time required: 1 hour round trip to get there from Page, including transit by 4WD vehicle to the canyon's entrance, plus 1 hour minimum inside the canyon.

Lower Antelope Canyon

The Young family has done a tremendous job installing a series of metal ladders to facilitate your descent into the Canyon. They have also installed a series of strategically placed emergency nylon ladders that can be dropped from above in an emergency. Because it is such a narrow canyon, you may find pockets of mud at any time during the year. If you want to explore the lower part of the canyon, bring a pair of sandals or, better yet, a pair of boots that you do not care too much about. Your boots will be a mess when you come out of the canyon.

The importance of respecting the dangerous forces of nature was tragically illustrated in August of 1997, when the lives of 11 French and Swiss tourists were lost in Lower Antelope Canyon. The visitors were descending in the company of a Navajo guide when a violent storm struck about 8 miles to the southeast at an altitude of about 2,000 feet. The Navajo guide told the tourists they would have to leave and they reluctantly complied, disillusioned at having to turn back after having come so far. On returning to the surface, the group, seeing that it wasn't raining, demanded to go back down against the warnings of the guide. A few minutes later the group was literally swept away by a wall of water over 30 feet tall spouting from the narrow passage, drowning the unfortunate tourists and carrying away their bodies towards Lake Powell in a torrent of mud. There were eleven dead and two badly injured survivors. It was many weeks before all the bodies were recovered from the debris and mud. The last two were finally found in November 1997.Always follow your guide's instructions as flash floods are frequent and it doesn't necessarily have to be raining in the canyon. This is true for all the slot canyons or narrows mentioned in this book. You should never risk going into a canyon if a storm is threatening close by, which is to say anywhere within a 10 mile radius.

Getting there: the road leading to Lower Antelope Canyon is located almost opposite the entrance to the Upper canyon and is well marked. The entrance is 1/2 mile further

Lower Antelope Canyon has some exquisite shapes

Time required: If you are serious about your photography, you may very well end up spending half a day or longer inside the canyon. Take some food and plenty of water. It can get unbearably hot and stifling during the summer months and very cold in the winter, especially if you decide to wade the mud holes.

Photo advice: photographing this canyon is great fun; it is also a tremendous challenge if you want to bring back photos of a high caliber. Variations of 5 or 7 f/stops are the norm and choosing the best exposure is not easy. Knowing your equipment well is a must: not only must you be able to operate it without hesitation, but you should be able to anticipate how your images will look. If there is one thing the author has learned from his many visits to Antelope, it is that experience can play an important role in increasing the number of high-caliber "keepers" that you'll bring back from your visit.

If you do not have a spotmeter, either hand-held or in your camera, be ready to bracket heavily: easily said when you shoot 35mm, but almost out of the questions if you carry a view camera. You'll often have to add 1 1/2 to 2 stops overexposure to bring out the detail on the darker surfaces without burning the lighter walls. If you add too much, what could be a beautiful yellow light could end-up totally white on that high-contrast slide film. Try to find compositions that restrict the EV range to the smallest possible range, avoid all the brightly lit areas, concentrating instead on reflected light. Take plenty of time to frame your shots. Take even more time to take your shots, use very small apertures and long pauses: let that beautiful reflected light seep onto your film. If you want the best possible results, have your film processed first, examine your results, learn from the inevitable mistakes and return to the Canyon. Be prepared to deal with a steady traffic of visitors who are not necessarily interested in photography and will be in your way. Just be courteous and don't take yourself too seriously and you'll find that people will give you a wide berth.

The best time to photograph Lower Antelope and obtain a rich palette of colors is from the early morning until about midday. Light becomes somewhat less interesting in the early afternoon.

Horseshoe Bend

Some 4 miles to the south of Page, the Colorado River forms a spectacular bend which provides a breathtaking view that you don't have any excuse for missing as it's so close to Page.

Getting there: leaving Page, set your mileage counter to zero when you pass the McDonald's and follow Route 89 to the south for 4.2 miles. A road veers off to the right towards a parking lot located a couple of hundred yards away. Coming from Page, the road is not marked—if you are coming from the south, there is a small sign saying "Scenic View"—but the parking lot is easily spotted. Park and follow the old 4x4 track to the bend, about half a mile further on.

Photo advice: the bend is very wide and requires a 24 mm or preferably a 21 mm lens. A 28 mm lens just won't do if you want to include both sides of the river. If you don't own an ultra wide-angle lens, then concentrate on a vertical composition taking in just one of the arms of the bend. The steepness is impressive, so try to include a bit of rock in the foreground to more accurately convey the depth of the canyon.

You'll get great results early in the day when the sun hits the Vermilion Cliffs on the horizon. A 2-stop graduated neutral density filter is a must to avoid having the sky and the plateau look washed out since the canyon will still be in shadows. At the end of the day, the view is equally splendid.

The view towards Lake Powell is also lovely. During the frequent thunderstorms, the sky is often a deep gray even though the sun bathes Tower Butte in a blaze of light. A 100 to 150 mm lens gives the best results.

Time required: 1 hour round trip to get there from Page, including the 1 mile plus round trip walk to the edge of the canyon. Allow at least 30 minutes at the canyon, more if you have time.

Water Holes Slot Canyon

Squeezing through the canyon

This spectacular slot canyon is really easy to get to and is worth a visit. Even though this canyon doesn't have the form and color of Antelope Canyon, it nevertheless has some nice formations and, as its name indicates, the water holes make it attractive.

If you are traveling during the tourist season, the visit will be more organized. Out of season, the gate is not manned and you'll have to pay a visit to the Navajo Parks and Recreation office (see Resources in the Appendix) to find a guide or, failing that, to get a back country permit.

You'll find an entrance cut into the barbed wire to the right of the gate. Don't follow the cairns towards the right (this will lead to a viewpoint of the canyon above the bridge) instead, head towards the electric pylons. In less than 700 feet, you'll come to a depression on the right that will allow you to descend very easily into the dry bed of the canyon.

Walk straight down the canyon in the direction of the bridge. After 500 feet, you'll find a superb steep wall about 150 feet tall with a narrow passage. The canyon is not very interesting beyond the bridge. Retrace your steps and walk upstream. At this stage, the canyon is still fairly large, but quite beautiful. About 1/2 mile further along you'll enter into lovely narrows where you'll catch sight of the first water pockets. Out-of-season, they're either dry or extremely muddy and make progress difficult. The narrows eventually turn into a slot canyon with beautiful walls and lighting effects. This visit is highly recommended if you don't have a chance to visit Little Wild Horse Canyon (see the chapter on San Rafael Reef).

Getting there: Water Holes Canyon is located 6 miles south of Page on Route 89. Its presence is first announced by a sign a few hundred feet before the entrance and by a second one just before the bridge spanning the Water Holes Canyon gorge. You can park on either side of the road.

Photo advice: this canyon is better lit than Antelope. However, a tripod is still needed to take shots of the rock texture. It's also an incomparable spot to get great photos of the family in the nooks and crannies of the canyon, or in one of the water pockets with water up to their thighs. An ISO 400 or 800 print film will let you take photos with a hand-held camera. The author has heard that you can get excellent views of the canyon from above just by following its edge, but hasn't been able to verify this.

Time required: 45 minutes round trip from Page, including the walk to the base of the canyon; 1 hour minimum in the canyon itself.

Buckskin Gulch Narrows

This fantastic mini-adventure in Buckskin Gulch will give a quick, but spectacular insight into the narrows of the Paria River, which crosses the Canyon/Vermilion Cliffs Wilderness. These are, for many, the most beautiful and interesting narrows on the Colorado Plateau.

The visit will take half a day, including the drive, and can easily be arranged when traveling between Kanab and Page. You can also do the Cottonwood Canyon Road on the same day (see the Grand Staircase/Escalante Chapter) since this comes out just a few miles from the Paria Canyon Visitor Center.

A trip to the Visitor Center is in order, not only to sign the register, but to get the latest weather information. Do not venture into Buckskin Gulch or Paria Canyon if bad weather is threatening. Once in the canyon, you won't be able to get out in case of flash floods. The enormous tree trunks lodged in the walls several feet above you testify to the force and height of the flash floods that can hit any time of the year, but particularly in summer.

From the Visitor Center, you can descend the Paria River from White Tank in a 10 mile round-trip. This will take a long day, and a large part of the walk will be in a dry wash that is not particularly interesting. Instead, your objective should be Buckskin Gulch. The best way to get there is from a location called Wire Pass.

The marked trail begins on the other side of the parking lot at Wire Pass and follows the dry bed of the wash about 3/4 of a mile before arriving at the entrance to the narrows. The first narrow, a few dozen yards long, will give a little preview of what awaits you further on. Soon, you enter the true narrows of Wire Pass and move along between very dark walls over a hundred feet high. You'll eventually reach the junction with Buckskin Gulch about 3/4 of a mile further on. Follow Buckskin Gulch straight ahead as long as you like or time permits.

Returning to the junction, go a little way up to the right into Buckskin Gulch instead of returning directly to Wire Pass. At this spot, Buckskin Gulch frequently contains water and mud holes, and will give you a good idea of what the narrows look like further down Buckskin Gulch and deep inside Paria Canyon.

Getting there: take the 89 from Page or Kanab and turn off at the sign that says "Visitor Center" to register and get a weather report. Unlike the nearby Coyote Buttes Wilderness, there is no quota limiting the number of dayhikers into Buckskin Gulch. Continue following the road, if you are coming from Page—or turn back if you came from Kanab—for about 2 miles until you come to a hard-packed dirt road branching off to the left when the main road makes a wide curve to the right. Be careful not to miss it as this dirt road is not clearly visible when coming from Page because of the angle and the fact it is slightly downwards from the road. Using this well-maintained track, pass Buckskin Trailhead at 4.3 miles and continue for another 4 miles to the parking lot at Wire Pass.

Photo advice: the narrows are generally rather wide, between 10 and 15 feet, with a narrow passage of about 3 feet at the entrance. They are also very high and therefore quite dark. They lend themselves better to group and individual portraits than to shots of texture or creative compositions. A wide-angle lens will let you maintain the depth-of-field and show the canyon's dimensions despite the wide aperture you'll be forced to rely on. Don't use a flash as this will wash out the foreground of the photos and create lots of unpleasant shadows. With a firm grip, it's perfectly possible to photograph with a hand-held camera using ISO 400 or 800 film. Also consult the general photographic advice at the beginning of this guide.

Time required: 1 hour round trip to get to Wire Pass from Route 89, 3 to 4 hours in the canyon to really enjoy it.

Coyote Buttes – The Wave

A few miles South of Buckskin Gulch lies one of the most extraordinary formations on the Colorado Plateau, an area of simultaneously gnarled, polished and twisted rock called the Coyote Buttes Wilderness Area. Within its Northern section lies its crown jewel: the Wave.

The Coyote Buttes wilderness area is a complex project jointly administered by the Arizona Strip Field Office, the Kanab Resource Area, the B.L.M, Northern Arizona University and the Arizona Strip Interpretive Association...did I forget anyone? Northern Arizona University handles the internet-only reservation system on behalf of the group. Concerns about widespread ecological damage to this pristine area has led to the establishment of a quota system in 1997, restricting visitation to twenty permits a day, evenly spread between the Southern and Northern sections of the Buttes. This means that only ten individuals can go to the Wave on any given day.

This drastically low quota may or may not be revised at some point in the future after studies show what impact a steady flow of visitors has on the land. The permits are issued for daytime use only and overnight camping is strictly forbidden within the Wilderness area.

Obtaining a permit for the Wave is a bit of a challenge: first, it requires that you have access to the internet, as it is the only way your reservation can be processed ; second the waiting list is such that you need to be very flexible when scheduling your visit.

Many people find the low quota system objectionable. The author does not have any moral or scientific authority to criticize it, but he is rather satisfied with the present system. A limit of ten bodies a day seems indeed quite low and you would think that

The Wave seen from the top

The narrow entrance to the Wave

doubling it would not have a major impact on the land. There are, however, several factors that weigh in favor of the low quota: the vast majority of visitors come to the Buttes to see the phenomenal site of the Wave and a concentration of visitors in this particular area not only could impact the fragile ecosystem but also would deter from the enjoyment of the place. Also, there are no trails within the wilderness area, except for a short jeep trail in the Northern section and the probability of inexperienced visitors getting lost and injured would increase exponentially without a quota. In fact, you would be well advised to have some prior cross-country navigation experience before venturing into the Buttes. While it is certainly possible to find your way to the Wave based on descriptions from friends or books and by looking for specific landmarks, it is not recommended that you attempt your first visit on your own. It is one place where a compass or a GPS will prove quite useful.

Getting there: you'll need to reserve your permit online well in advance by visiting the following web site : http://www.for.nau.edu/paria-permits/index.html. Depending on the time of year, you may have to browse the scheduling table for several weeks before you find an empty slot. Travelling as a group further decreases your chances of finding your date of choice. Be ready to make some scheduling concessions. From the Wire Pass trailhead, it is approximately 3 miles to the Wave. Count on 1 1/2 to 2 hours to reach the Wave, which is located on the Northern side of a large ridge called Top Rock. Top Rock comes into view to your right after you have cleared a ridge, about 45 minutes from the trailhead. It is easily identified by a long crack running vertically in its flank. Once you have found Top Rock and its crack, you will have no problem reaching the Wave. Just walk cross-country in that general direction, keeping as high as you can close to the ridge to your right. Coming back will be easier and shorter, because you'll be able to retrace your steps or avoid the detours and mistakes you made on the way in.

Photo advice: unless you have reserved on consequent days, which is allowed, you only have one day to explore the Buttes as no overnight camping is permitted within the wilderness area. The author found the best light to be in late afternoon, however the heart of the Wave itself will be plunged in shadows if you wait too long. Some of the colorful rock formations located to the right of the main corridor leading to the Wave are best photographed in the early morning. There is a myriad of details that can be photographed successfully throughout the day.

Reflections at the Wave

Rainbow Bridge

With a span of 275 feet, Rainbow Bridge is the largest natural bridge in the world. Its huge, albeit graceful, rounded curve of Navajo sandstone reminds one of Double Arch in Arches National Park. However, this bridge was formed by the action of water flowing from the slopes of nearby Navajo Mountain, a geologic process completely different from arches which are eroded by wind and rain. Considered a sacred place by the western Indians, it was very difficult to get to until the formation of Lake Powell. Today, you can easily reach it by boat from the various marinas on the lake.

Getting there: basically by joining an organized boat trip from the marina at Wahweap, located a few miles north of Page. The concessionaire organizes visits all year long. From May to September, it's also possible to get there from the Bullfrog Marina (see Capitol Reef and Glen Canyon). From the dock, you reach the viewpoint by means of a half mile long trail. You can also get there on foot from inland, with or without a Navajo guide, leaving from Rainbow Lodge, but this requires two long days.

Time required: 6 hours round trip. Obtain information on departure times in town or at the Visitor Center near the dam.

Magnificent Rainbow Bridge

Marble Canyon and Lee's Ferry

Crossing Route 89A's Navajo Bridge to Marble Canyon offers an excellent opportunity to stop, observe and photograph the Colorado at close range as you'll be about 450 feet above the river, which at this point flows slowly between two precipitous walls.

The descent to the edge of the Colorado River at Lee's Ferry—site of an old ferry used in the last century by travelers to cross the Colorado—is also interesting. It's the only chance to get down to the edge of the Colorado for miles around, except for descending on foot into the Grand Canyon (see the Grand Canyon Chapter) or going up to Moab. Strange rock formations, interesting to photograph, flank the left side of the road as it descends near Lee's Ferry.

Today, Lee's Ferry is essentially a marina for launching flat-bottomed fishing boats. If you visit Horseshoe Bend (see above), you're bound to observe one of these boats going upstream in the direction of Glen Canyon dam.

Getting there: Marble Canyon is right on Route 89A between Jacob Lake and Page. It's easy to include after a visit to the North Rim of the Grand Canyon. Lee's Ferry is 5 miles from the fork with 89A, on a paved road.

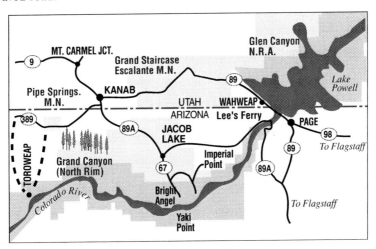

Getting to Page/Grand Canyon

Monument Valley from Artist's Point

Chapter 9
MONUMENT VALLEY

The Navajo Tribal Park

Monument Valley—or Tse' Bii' Ndzisgaii as the Navajos say—is the symbol par excellence of the American Southwest. Used hundreds of times as a backdrop for films and video clips, seen in innumerable TV and magazines ads, Monument Valley has become a kind of "transitory object" of humanity's collective psyche. Its subliminal imagery invokes a powerful associative reflex. The entire world intuitively knows that such a landscape only exists in the American West. A simple image, a profile on the horizon is enough to make us dream of great spaces, infinite possibilities, and escape from the daily grind and worries of our lives. Even its audacious name "Monument Valley"—who would think of calling a piece of the planet such a name—somehow conjures up a prehistoric world patrolled by dinosaurs. In any case, whether it's dreams or products, Monument Valley delivers.

The visit to Monument Valley won't disappoint you and you'll get your money's worth for the dream that made you come here in the first place. Everything is here just as you envisioned it: the hundreds of miles to get there, the long rectilinear ribbon of the road seen glimmering in the heat waves miles ahead and the fantastic monoliths profiled on the horizon. But it's no longer just a vision...you are now living the dream.

The visit to this park administered by the Navajo Nation begins at the Visitor Center where your gaze embraces a scene of extraordinary beauty over the valley and the landmark buttes of West Mitten, East Mitten and Merrick. These buttes, like the majority of formations in Monument Valley, look like a block of blond sandstone that's been cut with a sharp knife, covered by a hard, protective layer, while friable shale forms the base. This geologic combination gives these buttes their characteristic stair-step effect produced by the scree of the shale bed leading to a deep-cut mass that is protected on the summit.

To get the most out of Monument Valley, and bring back quality photos, you have to spend a bit of time and descend by car into the valley. A 17 mile circuit will lead you into the middle of the monuments, passing by some extremely photogenic spots along the way. The road is a bit rough on the descent, but it becomes much easier later on, so don't hesitate.

For the author, the best and most complete way to visit Monument Valley is to make two forays inside the park: the first in the afternoon in the company of a private Navajo guide and the second early in the morning in your own car.

A visit in the company of a private guide offers great flexibility and allows you to penetrate much further into the valley than with just your car, and to go around Thunderbird Mesa, the mesa just south of Rain God Mesa. This allows you to see various arches and get very close to the Totem and Yei-bi-chei, so they can be photographed with the dunes in the foreground. This is otherwise impossible from the scenic turnoffs of Totem Pole and Sand Springs where the dunes are almost invisible. The guide can also take you behind Mitten and Merrick

The Totem Pole and Yei-bi-Chei

buttes allowing you to vary the angles and lighting effects. In addition, the guide may offer you a visit to a hogan—the traditional Navajo home built of wood and topped with clay—where you can meet Navajos in traditional costume working at their weaving looms.

The "classic" view from Hwy. 163

Early in the morning, familiar now with the circuit road and the layout of the place, you can take your time to return and photograph the valley.

Outside the park, coming from Kayenta, you'll encounter a gigantic conical monolith on the right. This is Agathla Peak, better known as El Capitan. The mass of El Capitan makes a sensational photograph, captured with a telephoto lens from about a mile away on either side depending on the time and angle of the sun.

Getting there: coming from Page or Tuba City on the 160, take US 163 towards Kayenta; from Moab by the 191, turn onto US 163 right after Bluff. A 4-mile long paved road takes you to the Visitor Center.

Except after a rain, the valley road poses no problems for passenger cars or campers. In front of the Visitor Center, you'll find half a dozen concessions offering organized tours of the park. Group visits don't offer the same flexibility

The awsome sight of "El Capitan"

as one in the company of a private guide.

Photo advice: there are plenty of things to photograph and happily, the beginning of the morning and end of the afternoon are both interesting. However, the afternoon is always preferred since colors are very warm and sunsets can be absolutely unreal if you are lucky enough to have clouds. If you only do the Scenic Drive circuit, you'll feel that you are missing out since signs at each stop remind you that walking around is prohibited. This is very discouraging since you'll really want to get closer to the formations (in particular the dunes at Totem). If the sky is cloudless, it's only at sunrise or sunset that you'll get good photos, but a blue sky with thick white clouds will let you get good results all day long. Finally, a stormy sky towards evening with a few sunrays on the buttes is ideal.

The perspectives are extremely varied and you'll be constantly changing focal lengths. A zoom lens will prove extremely useful. A very wide angle lens (28 mm minimum, 24 mm preferred) is necessary to photograph the three buttes from the Visitor Center. A short telephoto can isolate each butte and eliminate the shadow zone produced by the vast mesa on which you are standing. The ideal time to photograph is in the evening as the setting sun embraces the buttes, but you can also get great backlit shots of the buttes profiled against a blue and red-charged sky by coming back just before dawn.

Merrick Butte, another"classic"

On the Scenic Drive, the loop made by the road around the Rain God Mesa will let you adapt to the lighting conditions. You can photograph just as well in the morning as in the evening. After leaving the Visitor Center, the road descends in switchbacks to the valley below. It's possible to get some lovely shots of the buttes from a wide opening located at one of the bends in the road, or from the dunes situated at the bottom of the descent.

John Ford's Point offers an excellent view of the Three Sisters group. You can capture it with a short telephoto lens, preferably in the morning since you would be shooting against the light in the afternoon.

In the morning, you can get a very nice photo of the Hub with a long telephoto lens that will compress the area between the Navajo hogans situated in front of the Hub with Weatherhill Mesa in the background.

The scenic turnoffs of Totem Pole and Sand Springs lead to two remarkable views of the Totem, Yei-bi-chei and the dunes. A 135 to 200 mm lens is necessary to photograph them, preferably in the warm light of afternoon. The Sand Springs viewpoint offers the best angle to photograph the Totem.

Further ahead, be sure not to miss Artist's Point for a fantastic panorama of the valley using either a wide-angle or a telephoto lens. It's particularly spectacular at the end of the afternoon. Finally, the stop at North Windows offers a superb view of the Mittens that you can frame in the "window" that opens in front of you.

Between Artist's Point and North Window, you have a very nice perspective over the Three Sisters, very different from what you saw at John Ford's Point an hour earlier.

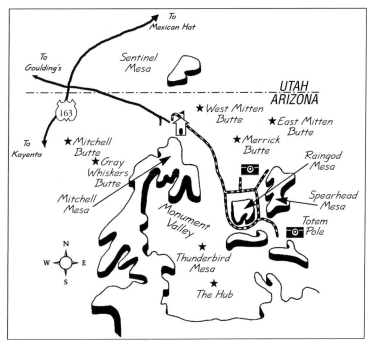

Monument Valley Navajo Tribal Park

Finally, you have probably read or are aware of the fact that it is forbidden to photograph the resident Navajos without their permission. You can usually find some Navajos at the main viewpoints who will pose for a modest sum. During summer, tours organized by the Gouldings Trading Post will allow you to photograph costumed Navajos posing for the tourists....if this is what you want.

Time required: 1 and 1/2 hours if you are in a hurry and can only stop at the Visitor Center to admire the panorama, linger a bit in the boutique or bargain for jewelry in the Navajo stalls located at the entrance to the park. Allow 1 and 1/2 to 2 hours for the Scenic Drive. Finally, plan on a day and a night if you want to photograph in the morning and the evening. For this you can stay at Kayenta or, even better, at the luxurious Goulding's Trading Post, just a short distance from the park.

Goosenecks State Park

Only about 20 miles north of Monument Valley, there is a little Utah state park largely ignored by travelers, still in a euphoric state from their visit to Monument Valley and in a great hurry to get to Arches and Canyonlands. The author has sent a good number of travelers to Goosenecks State Park and all of them, without exception, have come back raving about it.

It's only at the edge of the canyon that these goosenecks can be seen and they won't fail to surprise you. Here, the San Juan River has cut out four successive bends over 1,500 feet in depth in a shale core, twisting and turning for more than 5 miles in a space of less than a mile. This view is more remarkable for its oddity than for sheer beauty. You are presented

A gooseneck of the San Juan

with a geological phenomenon that defies the imagination. It's the kind of view of which we say "you have to see it to believe it". Go there and you won't regret it.

Getting there: 4 miles north of Mexican Hat on Route 163, turn at the sign for the park. Follow the narrow paved road for another 4 miles as it winds through the middle of the plateau.

Photo advice: the goosenecks make for an excellent picture no matter what size of wide-angle lens you have. There's no way you can get them all into one single shot anyway.

Time required: 1 hour round trip from Route 163.

Valley of the Gods

Just a few minutes away from Goosenecks State Park, you'll encounter an interesting track administered by the B.L.M. forming a loop around the place known as the Valley of the Gods. Strewn about the valley are imposing monoliths, quite different from those found at Navajo Tribal Park. Though quite beautiful, this valley doesn't offer the same photographic variety of the latter. The main advantage of the Valley of the Gods is that it is much less visited and an impression of solitude reigns here. You'll truly have the impression that you are embarking on an adventure, which is not the case in the highly controlled world of the Navajo Tribal Park.

The track is 17 miles long and is generally passable by passenger cars and small-sized campers.

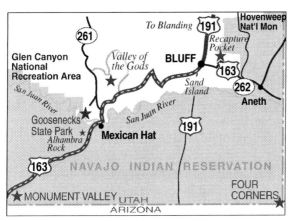

Getting to Monument Valley

Getting there: from Route 163, 8 miles northwest of Mexican Hat (4 miles from where it branches off Route 261 climbing to Natural Bridges). The track begins to the left of the road and is marked by a sign. You can also take the road in the opposite direction from the 261 and this is a preferred alternate in the afternoons.

Photo advice: you won't be disappointed by these Gods, immense monoliths rising high into the sky by the side of the track. The prettiest part is at the beginning of the track, taking it in the recommended direction.

Time required: 1 hr just to drive the loop, but 2 hr if you want to do it without rushing to take your photos.

Mokey Dugway and Muley Point

If you go up to Natural Bridges National Monument—or if you're coming down from there—by way of the Trail of the Ancients (Route 261), you'll be driving an amazing route that was carved into the flanks of the cliffs during the 1950's for the use of the uranium mines nearby. It's a gravel road along the 3 miles of hairpin turns climbing to the top, but it's wide and doesn't present any problems. You reach the top about 1,000 feet further up, at an altitude close to 6,000 feet, at the place called Mokey Dugway. Here you'll have a spectacular view of the Valley of the Gods. Monument Valley is also visible in the distance to the southwest.

A bit higher up on the plateau, a road about 3 miles long takes you to the viewpoint at Muley Point, offering an impressive panorama of San Juan canyon and Monument Valley in the distance.

Photo advice: these landscapes are so incredibly vast that it is easier and probably more interesting to simply admire them than to photograph them.

Navajo National Monument

This National Monument harbors some lovely Pueblo ruins tucked under overhanging sandstone cliffs. Still, the place is not comparable with Canyon de Chelly and Mesa Verde. If you are planning to go to either, then a visit to this spot is unnecessary. If it's your only chance to see some Pueblo-style dwellings, then don't miss it.

Getting there: by an excellent road, 9 miles long from the turnoff of Route 160.

Time required: 1 and 1/2 hours, including the short walk to the Betatakin viewpoint. Visiting the main ruins at Betatakin can only be done once a day on a ranger-led tour. It will take 4 to 5 hours (only from May to September).

Photo advice: the canyon at the bottom of which lie the ruins is quite steep and you'll have to wait until mid-morning to have any sun. There is good light radiating from the left in mid-afternoon, but don't wait too long because the main ruins with the best relief are located to the left in the bend of the arch and they'll be in shadow later in the day.

A 50 to 70 mm lens is perfect to take in the entire sweep of the ruins and the arch. A 100 mm lens is the minimum necessary for a close-up of the ruins.

Navigating Glen Canyon National Recreation Area

Chapter 10
AROUND GLEN CANYON

This chapter encompasses, in a very general way, the Blanding/Hanksville axis that allows you to get quickly from Monument Valley to Capitol Reef, leaving Moab for later.

For the purposes of this narrative, we'll be covering this route in an east-west direction that will basically allow us to follow along with the sun at our backs instead of in our faces.

Edge of the Cedars State Park

If you're arriving from the north, and haven't already passed through Monument Valley and Arizona, Blanding will be your first contact with the Navajo community that makes up 40% of the population of this unremarkable little town located at the foot of the magnificent Abajo Mountains. The lovely Edge of the Cedars museum, however, merits a stop as it's an excellent way to learn about the pre-Columbian Anasazi culture and also about the modern Navajo (Dineh) and Utes (Ncuc). There are some Pueblo-type ruins behind the museum which were inhabited until about 1220 A.D. They are moderately interesting but pale in comparison with those in Navajo National Monument or Canyon de Chelly. They do, however, give you a chance to descend into a reconstructed kiva. It's the museum that's the most interesting part of the Edge of the Cedars, so stow away your gear and devote an hour of your time to the visit. You won't be sorry you did.

Getting there: the park is in the town of Blanding on Route 191 and to get there is a bit like following the yellow brick road as you are guided to the museum by a series of Anasazi icons painted on the surface of the paved road.

Time required: 1 hour.

The Road to Hite

The road from Blanding to Hite, which partly follows the Trail of the Ancients, is absolutely spectacular and little used except in the summer months. At that time, you'll encounter a lot of motorhomes hauling boats in the direction of the Hite marina, the northernmost of the four marinas on Lake Powell.

A little after Blanding, you'll pass the Butler Wash Ruins and Mule Canyon on the right, practically on the side of the road. These ruins are not particularly interesting and the access is basically arranged to satisfy the curiosity of passersby who are in a rush. The really superb Anasazi ruins are found in the surrounding canyons and provide easy and magnificent walks. However, these ruins are located on B.L.M.-administered land and are not patrolled. It's apparent that the influx of visitors is having a detrimental effect on the preservation of these sites. If you are interested in Anasazi sites, consult the two works already cited in this text: <u>Hiking the Southwest's Canyon Country</u> by Sandra Hinchman and <u>Hiking Guide to the Colorado Plateau</u> by Michael Kelsey.

Passing the great rectilinear wall of Comb Ridge, which spreads over dozens of miles from north to south, the road gains elevation and crosses a vast juniper forest. The views of the Abajo Mountains to the north and the Henry Mountains to the northwest are spectacular.

Beyond Natural Bridges National Park, the rest of the way follows spectacular White Canyon, dominated by the

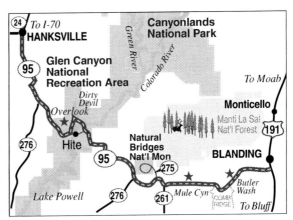

Getting to Glen Canyon

monoliths of Cheese Butte and Jacob's Chair. It's possible to descend into the canyon by a road on the left, about 2 miles after the sign for Jacob's Chair.

Crossing Lake Powell

You can cross Lake Powell in two ways. The main, most frequented route, is the 95 going straight towards Hite, passing Natural Bridges National Monument. You can also take Route 276—the old Hole-in-the-Rock Trail of the Mormon pioneers (see the chapter Grand Staircase/Escalante)—slanting due west to catch the ferry at Hall's Crossing and rejoin the Notom-Bullfrog road leading to Capitol Reef.

In the first instance, arriving at Hite Crossing, you'll leave the marina to the west and cross in succession the Colorado and the Dirty Devil River in the middle of an amazing landscape of petrified dunes.

After 2 miles on the north shore, you arrive at a viewpoint overlooking Lake Powell and affording an exceptional vista. Past the viewpoint, the road begins its climb to the north, crossing a superb canyon of Entrada sandstone in the vicinity of Hog Springs, where it changes to Navajo sandstone. It would be difficult to find a prettier spot. This area has a number of little side canyons waiting to be explored.

Getting there: from Blanding to Hanksville by the superb Route 95. From Blanding to Capitol Reef by Route 276 and the ferry. The John Atlantic Burr leaves Hall's Crossing every two hours between 8 a.m. and 6 p.m. in summer, between 8:00 a.m. and 4:00 p.m. in fall, and

Lake Powell near Hall's Crossing (Photo by Gene Mezereny)

8:00 a.m. and 2:00 p.m. in the winter. It leaves on the odd hours from Bullfrog between 9 a.m. and 5 p.m. The service is generally interrupted for maintenance in February. Always verify the schedule when you are near the Hall's Crossing marina by calling (801) 684-7000.

Phantom ship on Lake Powell (Photo by Steve Berlin)

Time required: 1/2 day for the drive, but it would be a shame if you didn't allow enough time to visit the magnificent Natural Bridges National Monument.

Natural Bridges National Monument

This National Monument is often passed by, not only because of the additional mileage it requires—and thus the delay this imposes—but also because many visitors incorrectly assume that it's some sort of second-rate Arches, which is not the case at all. This wonderful little park can be visited quickly and has a personality all its own. Natural bridges are eroded by the action of water flowing from rivers as opposed to arches which are eroded by wind and sand.

The three gigantic natural bridges here—Sipapu, Kachina and Owachomo—are spectacular. Because of their particular geological origin, they are set deeply inside canyons, instead of being in the open like arches. This makes the bridges difficult to photograph from the top of the canyon, but if you take the time to go to the bottom you'll be rewarded by superb views of these huge bridges. Sipapu is the longest, with a span of 286 feet, and is without doubt the most elegant of the three. It requires a descent of about an hour into the canyon to reach it. Kachina is the most impressive for its size. Being just a bit shorter than Sipapu, it is most notable for the extraordinary thickness of its span. Just under 100 feet thick, it resembles a gigantic rock muscle stretched 130 feet above your head. Owachomo is very easy to reach, which is a good reason for not missing it, though it is dwarfed in comparison with the other two.

Owachomo Natural Bridge

Getting there: from Monument Valley by way of Route 261, with the added bonus of the beautiful viewpoints of Mokey Dugway and Muley Point. Or, by the superb Route 95 leaving from either Blanding or Hanksville. These two roads between Blanding and the San Juan River form the Trail of the Ancients.

Photo advice: the Canyon is of a very ancient, light-colored Cedar Mesa sandstone, which is difficult to expose on a sunny day. It isn't easy to photograph the bridges from the road as they have a tendency to blend into the canyon. You'll have to find a way to isolate them, preferably against the sky, to convey the true measure of their size and the feeling of power which they project when close. There is only one way to do this, and that's by descending into the canyon. If you decide to do this, you're most likely to do so at Owachomo, where the bridge is located only a few minutes from the road. In that case, don't stop when you arrive at the bridge, but follow the trail going under it and to the left, descending towards the creek flowing below. The creek makes a nice foreground and the angle you'll get from below provides an easy exposure of the bridge throughout the day.

Time required: 2 to 3 hours in the park; add a half day to the trip if you decide to make this detour from Route 191 between Monument Valley and Blanding.

Wilson Arch, South of Moab

Chapter 11
AROUND MOAB

If there's one town in the west that has changed drastically in the last twenty years, it's Moab. The author knew Moab in 1975 when it was still a small hamlet with a couple of stray motels, a few odd restaurants and certainly no liquor. Today, Moab has become a cosmopolitan Mecca for tourists where they can buy cool bumper stickers saying "Paris, London...Moab" and relax after a long day of rafting or mountain biking in one of the two micro-breweries in town.

Moab is certainly the jumping-off spot par excellence for those two scenic giants of the Colorado plateau, Arches and Canyonlands. However, the area around Moab contains quite a few remarkable sites that would be a shame to miss. This chapter deals with those sites that don't quite have the stature of National Parks and Monuments, but can be just as fascinating and full of photographic opportunities.

Photo advice: Moab deserves special mention in a photographic itinerary. It's quite probable you'll be spending at least two nights in the area of Arches and Canyonlands. This would be a good time to get your film processed and check out your photos. There are several photo labs in town that can process color negative film and print photos in one hour. For E-6 processing and professional quality enlargements, there's only one place: Westlight Photography. You'll find Westlight on South Main Street if you turn left just before the Comfort Inn, a bit before the exit south of town. Westlight can process slide film in 3 hours and their work is impeccable. They'll deliver directly to your motel, after 7 p.m., the films you brought in before 4 p.m.. In summer, this will let you see your day's work before going back to Arches to catch the sunset. Westlight also carries a variety of film in cold storage. If you're badly in need of Ektachrome, Velvia, or Provia, it may be the only place in the whole region where you can stock up. Norm Shrewsburry, the proprietor of Westlight, is also a renowned professional photographer, specializing in action photography. Check out his beautiful work adorning the walls of the shop.

The Fisher Towers

The author strongly recommends this car trip that follows the steeply banked twists and turns of the Colorado River, stopping to photograph the impressive mesas of Castle Valley. You'll eventually come out on the magnificent plain of Professor Valley with the La Sal Mountains on your right, the Colorado River in the background and the Fisher Towers rising almost a thousand feet high in front of you at the far end of Richardson Amphitheater. These monoliths are extremely photogenic at sunset when the walls become almost completely red for just a minute or two. In the entire Colorado plateau, you'd be hard put to find a spot more red than this one. You'll find an interesting little group of goblins and chimneys to the right of Route 128, just after you pass the track leading to the Towers.

Getting there: at the north end of Moab, take Route 128 heading for the Colorado River and drive 5 miles past the Castle Valley sign. The

A close-up view of the Fisher Towers

The Fisher Towers reflecting in the icy Colorado River at sundown

track leading towards the Towers is marked and generally in good condition. To photograph the Towers with the river in the foreground, follow the 128 for about 3 miles, passing the Middle Bottom recreation area to the left. At this point, the Colorado River makes an elbow to the left. Follow this for about a mile until you can park on the left side of the road.

Photo advice: some local professional photographers have produced beautiful shots of the Fisher Towers with a full moon in the background. If you photograph the Towers just before they are in shadow, you can keep the exposure within a one-stop range of exposure values over the entire picture and get a perfect shot of the moon in the deep blue sky. It's also possible to get stunning vertical shots of the Towers from the edge of the river with a medium telephoto lens, using their reflection in the water as a foreground. A polarizing filter is a must to control the amount of reflection. To get this shot, you'll need to descend to the edge of the river and beat your way through the undergrowth. There is a flat rock miraculously placed in the river close to the bank, though you'll have to stretch your legs to get to it. From this precarious vantage point, you get an awesome view of the Towers. Look for that solitary rock from the bank. You shouldn't have too much trouble locating it, but getting to it is another matter.

Time required: 2 hours round trip.

The La Sal Mountains Loop

This magnificent 65 mile loop passing by the base of the La Sal Mountains offers a remarkable variety of landscapes, from alpine lake to canyons. A number of viewpoints along the roadside will let you photograph the summits, the pine forests, the canyons above Moab, and the Moab fault in the background. It's hard to beat that. The loop rejoins Route 128 just after the lovely little community of Castle Valley,

The Priest and the Nuns, near Castle Rock

at the foot of the towering monoliths of Castle Rock, the Nuns and the Priest.

Getting there: from the north, see the road description to the Fisher Towers. From the south, drive 6 miles south of Moab on Route 191 to catch the clearly marked loop. The upper part of the loop is closed or impassable in winter.

Photo advice: the preferred route in the morning is from the south and in the afternoon, from the north.

Time required: 2 1/2 hours to 3 hours.

Behind the Rocks

This place, often frequented by the locals, is a bit off the beaten path, but offers some excellent photographic opportunities. It has some superb goblin and fin formations of Entrada sandstone and the close presence of the La Sal Mountains in the background lets you compress them into the scene with a telephoto lens.

A 4x4 vehicle is needed if you want to go deep into Behind the Rocks from the south. However, it's also possible to get to some superb sites by foot from either end of the road.

The easiest and most spectacular access is the southern one. From there, you can easily reach a wonderland of rocks called Conehead Valley. The remarkable monoliths there, in the shape of conical skulls, make for some very interesting photos.

In the northern part of Behind the Rocks, you'll find the Pritchett Canyon trail leading to a natural bridge of the same name, at the end of Kane Creek Road. From the top of the canyon, you'll have a magnificent view of Behind the Rocks.

Getting there: for Pritchett, take Route 191 south and exit at Kane Creek Road just a few miles from Moab. Park in the lot by the side of the paved road and climb Pritchett Canyon to the top, a little under 10 miles round trip.

For Conehead Valley, follow Route 191 south a little more than 12 miles from the McDonald's in Moab. You'll come across a track leading off to the right. Watch out as this road is not posted and is easy to miss. The track can be driven with a passenger car for the first 1/2 mile or so and will let you get near Conehead Valley. It's preferable to park alongside the road where it begins to get worse and continue on foot to reach the Coneheads.

Time required: 2 hours round trip from the intersection with the 191 to get to Conehead Valley; 3 to 4 hours round trip to go up to Pritchett Arch.

Wilson Arch

See an arch without leaving your car? Easy enough. Twenty four miles south of Moab, you'll find Wilson Arch right next to Route 191. But if you want to climb to the arch to admire the beautiful view of the Abajo Mountains, prepare yourself for a rough ascent (about 150 feet of elevation gain in just 600 feet of trail). The descent on the slippery slickrock is even more difficult. Be extremely cautious. Afternoon is the best time to photograph the arch.

Cisco

Located at the end of Route 128, this microscopic hamlet—hardly more than a spot on the map—offers a foretaste of the plains character-istic of the western part of the state of Colorado bordering the Rocky Mountains. You wonder what the minuscule post office is doing here, lost in the middle of the plain while most of the other buildings are nailed shut with wooden planks. This place is in startling contrast with the red canyon landscape through which you have just come.

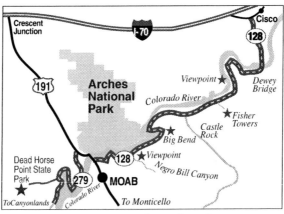

Getting to Arches and Moab

The Colorado National Monument

This national monument is pretty far away from Moab and it's diffi-cult to recommend unless you have a lot of time available. However, if you're going towards Grand Junction, perhaps on your way to Dinosaur National Monument or the Rocky Mountains, you'll pass right by it. In that case, this spectacular monument, located at the

Colorado National Monument in winter

extreme northern edge of the Uncompahgre plateau, strongly warrants a detour.

The Rim Rock Drive, forming a 23 mile loop, climbs the length of two gigantic arms of sandstone, gradually rising to about 1,000 feet above the valley. Many spectacular monoliths of Entrada sandstone can be seen from the plateau and in the proximity of the Visitor Center. The monument has recently become a favorite of climbers from all over the world.

The monument also contains innumerable dinosaur fossils.

Getting there: from Interstate 70, take Route 340 from Fruita or Grand Junction. The Monument is about 100 miles from Moab.

Photo advice: the west arm is the most spectacular, with a splendid view of Independence Monument and Pipe Organ at afternoon's end.

Time required: 2 hours in the monument, with stops at several viewpoints.

Delicate Arch at dusk

Chapter 12
ARCHES NATIONAL PARK

Almost everything has been written about Arches National Park in traditional guidebooks. What more can be said? That it's only been 30 years since it was an isolated and little-visited spot? That there was only a simple dirt track when Edward Abbey was a ranger there? Today, you're practically assured of finding a crowd rivaling that of the Grand Canyon, especially during the summer and on weekends.

With its extraordinary concentration of arches, this national park is incredibly spectacular and exercises a particular attraction for visitors from all over the world. The park can be visited year-round, though summer is without doubt the least interesting season. It's very hot and the long hours of sunshine make it difficult to photograph.

Park Avenue

This is your first contact with Arches National Park and an interesting stop. The best light is in mid-morning or afternoon.

The Petrified Dunes

These are some interesting Navajo sandstone formations, located close by the road and offering many photogenic compositions if you are interested and have the time.

Photo advice: If you wish to take photos off the beaten track, park in the lot before sunrise and walk in the direction of the dunes. Once there, walk for about 50 yards more into the heart of the dunes or until you come to a spot that seems picturesque and where you can't see your car. The sun rises behind the La Sal Mountains and directly lights the Great Wall, a series of rock faces several miles long that glow bright red with the appearance of the first sun rays. You can photograph these red walls with the petrified dunes in the foreground. A graduated neutral density filter is a must to preserve the detail of the dunes and still correctly expose the walls.

Balanced Rock

Often photographed, but still beautiful. You can see it close up by doing the 1/4 mile loop, but it also can be viewed far away from the Willows Flat trail.

Two views of Balanced Rock

Photo advice: you can photograph it from close-up with a wide angle lens or from the other side of the road with a 150 to 300 mm lens to isolate it against the backdrop of the La Sal Mountains and get rid of the cars and tourists. The end of the afternoon is best to do this. Night photos under a full moon give great results and are fun to shoot.

The Windows

This section of the park has a series of impressive arches that are easy to reach. From the parking lot, start your walk in the direction of Tur-ret Arch and the North and South Windows. Continuing past Turret Arch and South Windows, you'll come to a group of very interesting monoliths forming a great foreground with the La Sal Mountains in the background.

Back at the parking lot, cross the road to go to Double Arch where you can walk right under the double spans of this gigantic arch.

If you are lucky enough to be in Arches during the full moon, a night walk in this part of the park can be very rewarding. In summer, around midnight and under a full moon, the heat radiating from the ground and currents of

Behind the Windows

cool air mix in a delicious swirl around you and the rock formations of the Windows take on a fantastic quality.

Double Arch

Panorama Point

This spot provides a bird's-eye view of a good deal of the park, very lovely at the end of day, but too vast to be photographed with much success. You can, however, get a good morning view of Balance Rock and also of the Devil's Garden with a 200 to 300 mm telephoto.

The Fiery Furnace

The fins of the Fiery Furnace form an excellent foreground with the La Sal Mountains behind them. It's no longer possible to venture alone into this area—too many people have gotten lost in this maze of rocks. You are now required to join a guided walk in the company of a ranger. An extra fee is charged for the visit.

Photo advice: the visit is worth your while. If you don't have time to do the guided walk, you can descend for a short distance towards the fins to photograph them with a medium or long telephoto lens and compress the perspective.

You can also get an excellent view of the Fiery Furnace from Skyline Arch, just 300 yards from the road on a good path.

Devil's Garden and Landscape Arch

The walk into Devil's Garden is a real pleasure. It's an easy two mile walk to Double O Arch, passing Navajo Arch and the magnificent Landscape Arch along the way. You should do this walk early in the morning to capture the best light on Landscape Arch and to avoid the extreme heat of the day. A large block of rock recently fell from the 306 foot long span of Landscape Arch, causing the National Park Service to close the trail that went under the arch and allowed you to climb up behind it.

Photo advice: the arch is perfectly lit in the early morning during

Landscape Arch appears perilously close to breaking

summer, which allows you to capture the warm tones of the rock. The view in complete sunshine is only available in mid-morning during the rest of the year and a moderate warming filter will help restore the rich color saturation of the stone. The fence that was recently put up will severely limit your composition in framing Landscape Arch artistically. The best vantage point to photograph the arch against a background of sky is at the end of the short spur. It's interesting to note that the names Landscape Arch and Delicate Arch were reversed by error on the first printing of the map, and the names have stuck ever since. You can decide for yourself when you're there which names correspond best with the appearance of the arches.

Delicate Arch

Arches National Park, like the State of Utah, wouldn't be the same without the extraordinary symbol of Delicate Arch.

Delicate Arch is not easy to get to and that's just as well because it somewhat limits foot traffic, which is already very high. You can reach it by taking a trail that's about a 3 mile round trip, half of which is marked by the footprints of previous visitors on the slickrock as well as by strategically-placed cairns. Though it may be easy to climb to Delicate Arch during the day, it's another story to try and do this at night. Exercise extreme caution when descending after sundown. It's easy to take a bad fall if you tend to shuffle along and not lift your feet sufficiently.

It's not recommended you climb to Delicate Arch in the middle of the day. This is partly because the climb is hard and can be exhausting if the temperature is high, but also because the arch doesn't reveal all its splendor until dusk. You can get information in town as to when the sun will set and figure the best time to climb to it.

Photo advice: the lower part of the arch is in shadow at sunset in July and it's only at the beginning of winter that you can get the best shots with a warm light covering the entire arch. There aren't many angles to use at sunset. Backlit shots taken from the extreme left of the arch aren't very satisfactory and the view directly down the axis of the arch is only suitable for family photos. The best vantage point by far is from the edge of the rock ledge encircling the arch, where the trail comes out. Try to position yourself so that the highest peaks of the La Sal Mountains are profiled on the horizon between the base and the summit of the arch, a height of about forty feet. These peaks are frequently adorned with a rosy veil during the last moments of sunset when the arch is lit up in red. If you can, stay for thirty minutes after the sunset proper to capture the residual lighting in the clouds and just to appreciate this sublime spectacle while the rest of the crowd hurries toward the parking lot.

Delicate Arch Viewpoint

The road continues past Delicate Arch trailhead to a viewpoint of Delicate Arch. It's quite interesting to go there to see how precariously the arch rests on the plateau. This trip should preferably be made before the end of the afternoon.

You reach the upper viewpoint at the end of a moderately difficult trail of about 1.3 mile round trip. The view of the arch and the cirque just below it are rather startling. Photographing the arch requires a long focal length: a 200 mm telephoto lens will isolate the arch perfectly, but anything above 100 mm will do. A 24 mm lens is necessary for a panoramic view of the cirque and to accommodate the butte to the right.

Delicate Arch seen from the lower viewpoint

The Klondike Bluffs

This little-frequented section offers excellent photo opportunities, particularly of Tower Arch, but also of the extraordinary fins of the Marching Men. This group can be easily observed with a pair of binoculars from Route 191 and appears quite near. However, you will have to get there by way of the "official" sandy, though very driveable, Salt Valley Road.

Getting there: it's possible, and also relatively easy, to leave the park (and also to enter) by following Salt Creek Road to the north until the intersection with Thomson Road. Turning to the left, you'll reach the 191 in less than a mile. The author has driven this road in a 4WD vehicle and feels it would present no difficulties for a passenger car when the weather is dry. As always, you must get directions in town or from the rangers to learn the exact condition of the road.

Photo advice: the Klondike Bluffs can be photographed early in the morning or late in the afternoon, but in the evening you'll be able to get the La Sal Mountains in the background.

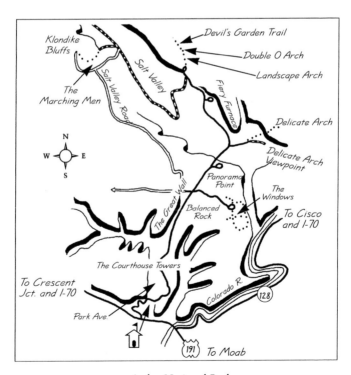

Arches National Park

Dead Horse Point at dawn

Chapter 13
CANYONLANDS NATIONAL PARK
(Island in the Sky)

Just twenty years ago this park received only 10,000 visitors a year. Today, though not as heavily visited as Arches, it's become the destination of choice for 4x4 enthusiasts, mountain bikers, and certainly for photographers. Unfortunately, it has also been discovered by Madison Avenue and Hollywood, and you can see it in more and more movies, TV ads and music videos. This may have a very negative impact on the park in the near future.

The author has made numerous visits to Canyonlands and heartily recommends it to those who love sweeping canyon panoramas, river goosenecks, and who wish to escape the Grand Canyon crowds. He has recommended and continues to recommend this park to innumerable visitors. They return unanimous in their opinion that the views are vaster and more impressive than those of the Grand Canyon.

Dead Horse Point State Park

If you do not have much time, go straight to Dead Horse Point State Park. This park, administered by the State of Utah, offers a fantastic panorama. It is the prototypical canyon of the American West as pictured in ads and movie westerns. Dead Horse Point is a bit like Monument Valley viewed upside down.

Getting there: by the excellent Route 313 which splits off Route 191 coming from Moab and going towards Interstate 70. Dead Horse Point State Park. is about 4 miles from where it splits with the road continuing to Canyonlands. Plan on 35 to 45 minutes from Moab. If you have a 4x4 vehicle, you can go back down by way of Long Canyon.

Photo advice: the best location is at Dead Horse Point Overlook, which offers two panoramas: the bend of the Colorado River with its superb mesa at the center and a view of the canyons with the La Sal Mountains in the background. From the parking lot, the choice of views is limited. Walk around the viewpoint and pick a foreground you like, which will best show the depth of the canyon and the immensity of the terrain. A 28 to 35 mm lens is ideal for the river bend. For the panorama of the canyon and the La Sal Mountains, you can give free rein to your imagination if you have a zoom. Any focal length will highlight something different. The bend is best photographed in the early morning, with the sun rising on the left, but sunset is equally beautiful. In fact, the subject is so awe-inspiring that even mid-day photos will be impressive. It's possible to photograph it before sunrise or after sunset using a warming filter to avoid a bluish tint on the mesa. On the other hand, for the panorama of the canyons, a morning or evening light is essential to best render depth and contrast. With a bit of luck and patience, the high clouds will be basking in the last gleams of sunset and the snowy peaks of the La Sal Mountains will be a vivid pink. You can also go to Basin Overlook for a slightly different view of the canyons. It's located about a half mile before Dead Horse Point when returning towards the ranger station.

Time required: 1 and 1/2 hour round-trip to get there from Moab and 1 hour on location. However, you will most likely want to visit this place at the same time as Canyonlands. The complete circuit—to Grand View Point—can be done in a long half day at a hurried pace, though that will mean sacrificing taking pictures at either sunrise or sunset.

Mesa Arch

Island in the Sky is the most accessible—and also the most visited— of the three sections of the park. The time is long gone when you had

The vast expanse of Island in the Sky provides tremendous depth

to get there on a dirt track that was almost always deserted.

Mesa Arch, located a short distance past the entrance to Island in the Sky mesa, offers an outstanding photographic opportunity. But there is a price to pay—you'll have to get up well before dawn if you want to catch it. If you go during the day, you'll see the entire superb spectacle of these immense canyons revealed through a magnificent arch perched on the edge of a precipitous drop...not bad, you say. Yes, but there's better still. How about a truly magical photograph? Here's the secret to shooting it successfully:

Start by getting the precise time of sunrise for that day. You can get this information the day before at Westlight Photography in Moab or from the park rangers. Plan to be at the Mesa Arch parking area about a half hour before sunrise. From Moab, plan on 45 minutes travel time to get there. Park your car and take the trail, you'll have a good fifteen-minute walk. There will still be 15 minutes, plenty of time to find a spot, prepare your equipment and try to visualize in your mind's eye the extraordinary spectacle that will soon be unveiled. Don't rush it, even if the sky is already very light. There will still be plenty of time before the sun actually appears and nothing will happen without its presence.

When the sun makes its appearance, far beyond the canyons, the underside of the arch will glow a vivid red, offering an absolutely sublime spectacle. The sun rises on the left of the arch in summer and on the right in winter. In either case, it's possible to frame it inside one of the arch's pillars.

You'll get the best results by setting your exposure on the sky just below the arch. If your camera doesn't have spot measuring, just trust your metering system and add a half stop overexposure to be safe. The author has always obtained the best results either with the normal exposure indicated by the camera or with a half stop of overexposure, but not more. You'll have a good fifteen minute window of opportunity to photograph the underside of the arch basking in intense red light, gradually turning orange and yellow on the edges. Work briskly, the first five minutes are the most intense. You'll have a hard time containing your excitement in the face of such a magnificent spectacle. For the grand finale, position yourself so the sun appears masked just behind the edge of the arch and bracket a couple of stops on each side. If you have company, you can ask them to take a back-lit photo of you on the arch. It makes for a fun shot. The arch is only 5 feet across...so exercise extreme caution as you'll be right next to a drop of several hundred feet. Warning: rangers have always discouraged visitors from walking on arches. It may have become official policy by the time you read this. Check with the rangers.

You'll get excellent results with lenses ranging from an extreme wide angle to 35 mm. A 35 mm lens will allow you to get better detail of the

Mesa Arch at sunrise

canyons through the arch and of the La Sal Mountains in the distance. A tripod is of course indispensable to maximize the depth of field. An artistic blur of the foreground or background would kill the impact of this classic landscape composition.

If you back up about 70 feet, a hillock will let you take shots with an 80 to 105 mm lens, compressing the perspective of the canyons and the La Sal Mountains with the incandescent top of the arch.

Mesa Arch can also be photographed successfully at the end of the afternoon with the sun lighting the front of the arch and the canyons in the distance. The accent is then on the contrast between the strongly lit arch and the very blue sky.

Grand Viewpoint

Grand Viewpoint offers such a breathtaking panorama that you won't regret the miles you've traveled to get to Canyonlands. Your eye encompasses hundreds of miles around. Unfortunately, it's not an easy task to capture this on film. The morning light is especially bad in the case of Grandview Point. Try to return at the end of the afternoon or in the early evening to photograph Monument Basin and White Rim to the west. This side is clearly more spectacular than the panoramas to be had from Green River Overlook and Murphy Point. Buck Canyon is worth a stop and gives a good vertical shot of the basin.

The Shafer Trail

The Shafer Trail lets you descend onto the White Rim plateau. It was originally an old cattle road that was enlarged in the 1950's during the uranium boom. You can observe its spectacular switchbacks carved right into the flank of the steep canyon cliffs from the Shafer Trail viewpoint, located a few hundred yards past the Visitor Center.

It's possible, but extremely risky, to attempt to descend the Shafer Trail in a passenger car. Some have tried and made it, but according to the Park Service, others have had to be hauled out with a tow truck. In any case, without a 4x4 vehicle you wouldn't be able to get further than the bottom of the canyon, which is still enough to scare you when you look back at the trail's switchbacks from below.

To get a close-up view of the Colorado River and the famous White Rim, you'll need a 4WD vehicle. It's easy to rent one for the day in Moab. In the course of a long summer day, you can watch the sun rise at Dead Horse Point, visit Island in the Sky, descend the Shafer Trail and spend a few hours on the White Rim, before returning to Moab by way of Potash finishing the day with a bit of off-road excitement.

Upheaval Dome

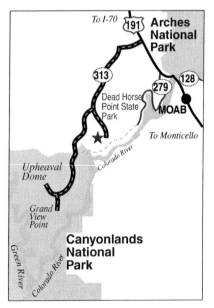

Getting to Canyonlands (Island)

This geologic phenomenon is quite interesting to observe but almost impossible to photograph. However, it would be a shame to miss as there's a paved road leading to it. The various geologic layers of the park are particularly well displayed and easy to observe because of the angle of the walls. It's a perfect opportunity for a little refresher course on the geology of the plateau and to learn to distinguish between the colors and the strata of the various sandstone formations.

The Dead Horse Point gooseneck and Shafer Trail

The White Rim Trail

For a visit in greater depth to the extraordinary White Rim and Monument Basin, you'll have to allow—and make reservations for—a trip of four days and three nights to cover the 125 miles of the loop. Cars can only take this road in one direction, and there is a quota system established by the National Park Service.

Though this adventure takes time, it is also unforgettable. Done in autumn or spring, you can take advantage of the long days without suffering from summer's heat or icy winter nights (on this arid plateau, night-time temperatures drop well below freezing in November).

The National Park Service issues a dozen permits a day, the maximum allowed by the number of primitive campsites located along the road. Some of these are unique, like that of White Crack, which has only a single car site. You will be alone on the edge of the canyon, the long ribbon of the Colorado River quietly flowing a thousand feet below. Island in the Sky dominates the horizon over a thousand feet higher and a magnificent starry sky serves as your roof. The immensity and solitude of the surrounding canyons is impressive. The only other human beings for over 40 miles around are the few at the other campsites scattered along the 125 miles of road. It's an unforgettable trip and, all in all, relatively easy to accomplish. The only negative point is that the National Park Service no longer allows wood fires on the

White Rim. This makes the long cold nights much less comfortable, especially in the off-season when it can become icy cold.

The most interesting section of the White Rim is without doubt Monument Basin, which you'll reach on the second day and where photographic opportunities abound. It's possible to make the round trip to Monument Basin in one very long day in a 4x4 vehicle in summer.

Getting there: see Dead Horse Point State Park.

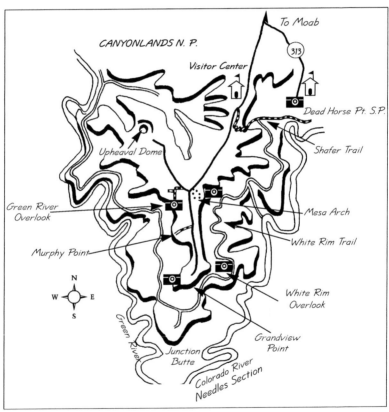

Island in the Sky

The Needles from Big Spring Canyon

Chapter 14
CANYONLANDS NATIONAL PARK
(The Needles)

The Needles section is much more difficult to get to and so is much less visited than Island in the Sky. Most of the difficulty lies in the distance there and back. It is in a cul-de-sac with only one way in and out. However, the travel distance is definitely worth your trouble, as you'll see.

The best way to visit the Needles is to camp at Squaw Flat. This will let you photograph these extraordinary needles in the early morning, while the light is at its best, before going to Chesler Park in the afternoon. If you can't camp, you can always resort to staying in a motel in Moab, Monticello or Blanding and, time and budget permitting, taking a plane flight over the Needles (see below).

Getting there: Moab offers all the advantages of modern civilization, but is 75 miles (about 1 and 1/2 hours) from the Visitor Center. Monticello can save you time as it's only 49 miles (or one hour) away. Also, this small town at the foot of the Abajo Mountains has a bit of an alpine appearance which is quite pleasant. As for Blanding, it's a hodge-podge of buildings without much charm, and it only makes sense to stay there if all the motels are full in Monticello, which is rare. Regardless of your starting point, you turn off Route 191 onto Route 211, almost opposite an interesting monolith called Church Rock, for the last 35 miles leading to the park.

If you get to the Needles before sunrise or after sunset, watch out for the great number of deer that are always crossing the road between the intersection with Route 191 and the Harts Draw fork. This last road allows you to make a shortcut from Monticello to Route 211 and the Needles. It's particularly impressive to see an adult buck coming at you from the side when you're traveling at 50 miles per hour. These animals have no sense of fear when they see your headlights and it is entirely up to you to avoid hitting them.

Photo advice: you'll find a lovely flat prairie at the intersection of the Scenic Route and Elephant Hill Road. It makes an excellent foreground for the view of the Needles in the morning or if you just want to observe them from the road with your binoculars.

Newspaper Rock

After passing by the base of the Abajo Mountains, the road follows the lovely, shallow canyon of Indian Creek, along which you'll stumble upon Newspaper Rock State Park. Even if you aren't a fan of Anasazi pictorial art, you really should stop to see these remarkable petroglyphs carved in the rock. A couple of them have been found to be 1,500 years old, but the majority were carved more recently over a period of several hundred years.

Newspaper Rock's inscriptions span several centuries

The Slickrock Trail

Once at the Needles, your first objective is to go by car to Pothole Point next to Big Spring Canyon Overlook. Pothole Point contains an interesting group of waterholes carved by erosion into the rock. Nearby, you can see some nice examples of cryptobiotic soil along the half-mile, one-way trail. Be sure not to step on it, as it literally takes decades to regenerate. Big Spring Canyon Overlook, at the end of the road, is a very lovely canyon with easy access, if you prefer not to do too much walking. Shortly before Big Spring Canyon Overlook, the 2.4 mile Slickrock Trail makes a loop along the mesa top overlooking the canyon.

Photo advice: if you don't want to walk all the way, the first viewpoint on the Slickrock Trail, a short half mile from the start of the trail, offers a great panoramic view of the cliffs

Potholes in the delicate cryptobiotic soil

with the La Sal Mountains in the background. There are miles of cliffs that glow red in the setting sun while the snowy peaks are tinted pink.

Squaw Flat

For a fantastic view of the Needles at sunrise, take the Big Spring Canyon trail from the Squaw Flat parking lot. In less than a mile, you'll come to a viewpoint overlooking the Needles. An 80 to 200 mm zoom lens would be perfect here, allowing you to get different shots with the rising sun striking the walls. A polarizing filter will help accent the relief and darken the sky a bit so that the needles will stand out perfectly.

After having photographed the sunrise from this viewpoint, you might want to follow the very scenic trail descending into Big Spring. It's an easy walk and the scenery is enchanting. A little under 3 miles down the trail, you'll come to a second viewpoint, even closer to the Needles. From there, you can best capture them using an 85 to 135 mm lens.

Elephant Hill

The Elephant Hill gravel road leads to a 4x4 track of the same name, as well as to the Elephant Hill foot trail. From the highest point on the road, you can get a superb panorama of the Needles section. A few hundred yards after the "blind curve" sign, you'll see a small slickrock hill to the right. You can easily climb on it for an excellent view of the entire area, including the Needles. The view is particularly majestic at sunset. Watch out for the cryptobiotic soil, however.

The 4x4 track is only for specially equipped vehicles and requires an excellent knowledge of driving on slickrock and of your vehicle's reactions. On the other hand, you can also go this route on foot or on a mountain bike for a short distance. It's very interesting to see the 4x4s negotiate the slickrock grades. The Elephant Hill 4WD track leads to the confluence of the Green and Colorado Rivers and also to Chesler Park

The Elephant Hill foot trail heads off in the opposite direction from the 4x4 track, but also ends up at Chesler Park and Druid Arch.

Chesler Park

This extraordinary group of spires with strongly colored striations is located behind the Needles that you see from the road. These extremely ancient spires of Cedar Mesa sandstone are located in the center of a remarkable verdant basin surrounded by a circle of needles. A second park, Virginia Park, is located a bit to the south and is also spectacular. The tall grasses surrounding these parks form a magnificent foreground and a singular contrast with the spires.

The Chesler Park Viewpoint can be reached on a slickrock trail that's not always easy to follow. It's a 6 mile round trip from the Elephant Hill parking lot. However, if you really want to get the most out of Chesler Park and take photos in late afternoon light, you'll have to descend into the park from the Viewpoint and make a loop of about 10 miles from Elephant Hill. This seems a bit long, but once in the park, you'll progress rapidly over flat ground and the loop can easily be completed in a 6 or 7 hour hike. This leaves plenty of time for pictures, rest and enjoying the scenery. Watch out for the heat and possible dehydration if you do this hike in summer. Even in late afternoon, the heat is still intense.

Photo advice: best early in the morning for the view of the Needles from the beginning of the trail and from Chesler Park Viewpoint, but afternoon is preferred for photographing the spires from the so-called Joint Trail, located behind Chesler Park.

Time required: about 3 hours round trip from the parking lot at Elephant Hill to the Chesler Park viewpoint and 6 to 7 hours to hike the loop via the Joint Trail.

Salt Creek and Angel Arch

You'll need a 4x4 vehicle for this pleasant, though nonessential trip. If you have one, or rent one in Moab, it's an easy drive in the dry bed of Salt Creek to go photograph Paul Bunyan's Potty and Angel Arch. This journey of about 22 miles round-trip currently requires a permit which you can get, simply by asking for it, at the Visitor Center.

Watch out for the extremely aggressive deerflies that patrol the Salt Creek bed during spring and summer.

Paul Bunyan's Potty

Above the Needles and the Maze

The best way to get an idea of this highly inaccessible section of the park is to survey it from a tour plane. A flight can easily be arranged from Blanding, Monticello or Moab. Better still, you can arrange to be picked up and dropped off on the landing strip adjacent to the Needles Outpost. Seen from a small aircraft, the landscape of the Needles and the Maze is extraordinary. A one hour flight allows you to view Salt Creek, the Needles, Chesler Park and Virginia Park, the confluence of the Green and the Colorado Rivers, Cataract Canyon and all of the fantastic formations of the Maze section. These include: the Doll House, the Land of Standing Rocks, the Chocolate Drops, Elaterite Butte, the Orange Cliffs, and more.

If you only take one small plane trip in the course of your journey through the Land of the Canyons, make it this one. You won't regret the money spent. Two people are necessary to book the flight. You can

Aerial view of Chesler Park

have three, but it won't change the price of the charter. Look in the chapter on Resources at the end of this book for information on local pilots.

Photo advice: a 28 to 50 mm lens is well suited to aerial photography of this area. Little or no depth-of-field is required, but you will of course need to keep the vibrations of the aircraft and your own movements in check. With slow film, an aperture of f/4 or 5.6 and a minimum shutter speed of 1/250 sec. represents the best compromise for sharpness and resolution. Ask the pilot if he'll allow you to have the windows open. If not, place the lens as close as possible to the window.

In any case, disengage the autofocus and manually set the focus for infinity.

The end of the day is ideal for color and relief, but if you leave too early you'll get very pronounced and sometimes unpleasant shadows.

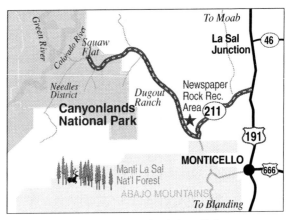

Getting to Canyonlands (Needles)

APPENDIX

Glossary

Arch: a natural opening eroded by the action of the elements (wind or rain). Not to be confused with a natural bridge which is formed by the action of flowing water.

Badlands: desert terrain forming strongly eroded shale or limestone hills, frequently striped with spectacular colors. Similar to the Badlands of the Dakotas, named "mauvaises terres" by French Canadian fur trappers.

Balanced Rock: a rock of hard material resting on top of a softer formation that has been eroded away, leaving the former balanced on top of the latter.

Butte: a small, deeply cut mesa that has been protected from erosion by a hard sedimentary layer on its summit.

Canyon: a deep gorge formed by the course of a river.

Fins: a group of individually eroded rocks similar in shape to the fin of a shark and following vertical fracture lines.

Flash flood: a torrent of water suddenly formed by a violent rainstorm falling on non-porous soil. On the Colorado plateau, these torrents naturally gravitate towards fissures in the rock, forming narrows and slot canyons.

Fold: a rise formed by the irregular uplift of sedimentary layers of rock. In the Waterpocket Fold, a layer located 6,000 feet deep inside the earth at its eastern end may be exposed as a surface layer in the west.

Goblins: formations of soft rock where erosion has resulted in grotesque forms, also referred to as Hoodoos. This term evokes images of mythological creatures of a grotesque shape.

Goosenecks: bends in a river in the form of loops or elbows.

Mesa: a fairly high plateau elevated above the surrounding plain. Its name means "table" in Spanish.

Natural Bridge: a natural opening formed by water action piercing through thin rock at the bend of a river.

Narrows: a canyon whose walls are extremely close, formed by a water course which is often dry.

Needles: hard or soft sandstone eroded in the form of jagged points by the elements, also called spires or minarets.

Reef: a natural rock barrier in the form of a ridge, formed by an almost vertical uplift of sedimentary layers.

Sand pipes: columns of light-colored rock of a phallic shape emerging in a haphazard manner from the earth.

Slickrock: generic term used to describe sandstone of the Colorado plateau on which it is difficult to get traction, such as the Slickrock Trail of Moab, a favorite of mountain bikers. This sandstone, polished by the elements, becomes extremely slippery under sand and snow.

Slot canyon: a narrow passage with smooth walls, formed not by constantly flowing water, but by the repeated action of flash floods.

Wash: an intermittent or seasonal water course, often the path followed by flash floods. A road crossed by a wash can become impassable after a storm.

Maps

The maps are classified by scale, beginning with the largest and most general.

Large scale road map: the best general road map is without doubt the "Indian Country" map published by the Automobile Club of Southern California. This remarkable map is a sheer pleasure to read and use. It helps in locating geologic phenomena such as the Grand Staircase or the Waterpocket Fold. For many years, it did not include the region of Arches and Canyonlands, an omission which has been rectified today on the back of the map. Unless you intend to do some heavy-duty hiking or fourwheeling, this map is quite sufficient for an ordinary car-based tour of the "Grand Circle". You can obtain this map from any AAA office and many of the shops in the National Parks and Monuments. This map is also available from this publisher, with or without our photography CD-ROM.

Note: the only site featured in this guidebook not covered by this map is the Colorado National Monument, located near Grand Junction, for which you will need a road map of the state of Colorado.

Detailed road maps: Southeastern Utah and Southwestern Utah maps are published by the Utah Travel Council. Roads and tracks are indicated in a very precise fashion. These maps can prove very useful when used in conjunction with the Indian Country map, especially to find less important 4WD trails.

National Park and Monument miniguides: these wonderfully concise mini-guides are packed with all the essential information about the parks, their history, geology and fauna. You can get them at the park entrances or at Visitor Centers. They will help you find your way around on roads and trails.

Topographic atlas: DeLorme Utah Atlas. A very well done resource (not used by the author).

National Park topographic maps: if you plan on adventuring along the trails and roads in distant parts of the national parks, the topographic maps of the Illustrated Trails series, printed on waterproof paper, are extremely well made and highly recommended. The author always uses them for hiking in the parks.

4x4 topographic maps: Fran Barnes' maps in the Canyon Country series are excellent. They are U.S. Geological Survey topo maps on which are superimposed the numerous and little frequented 4x4 trails. They are extremely practical if you travel with a 4x4 vehicle.

Bibliography

You have a wide selection of materials from which to choose among the traditional guidebooks, but the most remarkable reference work which is highly recommended to introduce you the National Parks is:

National Geographic's Guide to the National Parks of the USA, published by the National Geographic Society, (888) 225-5647

Some other recommended works:
Hiking the Southwest's Canyon Country by Sandra Hinchman, published by The Mountaineers Press, ISBN 0-89886-492-5

Canyon Hiking Guide to the Colorado Plateau by Michael Kelsey, published by Michael R. Kelsey Publishing, ISBN 0-944510-11-6

Hiking Utah by Dave Hall and Ann Seifert, published by Falcon Press, ISBN 1-56044-475-4

Hiking Zion and Bryce Canyon N.P. by Erik Molvar & Tamara Martin, published by Falcon Press, ISBN 1-56044-509-2

Exploring Canyonlands and Arches by Bill Schneider, published by Falcon Press, ISBN 1-56044-510-6

Scenic Driving Arizona by Randy Johnson & Stewart Green, published by Falcon Press, ISBN 1-56044-449-5

Scenic Driving Utah by Joe Bensen, published by Falcon Press, ISBN 1-56044-486-X

Canyon Country Off-Road Vehicle Trails (a collection) by Fran Barnes

Other Recommended Reading

The author cannot recommend too highly these four works he feels are essentials on the subject or surroundings of the Land of the Canyons. Reading these books during a trip in the American West reinforces the pleasure of discovery.

Mormon Country by Wallace Stegner, published by the University of Nebraska Press, ISBN 0803291256: a fundamental work on the colonization of Utah by the Mormons; impartial, remarkably documented and an easy read. It would be a shame to cross Utah without knowing or understanding the remarkable saga of the Mormon pioneers.

The Dark Wind by Tony Hillerman, published by Harper, ISBN 0061000035: a novel with a very cool Navajo cop as its reluctant hero. An excellent introduction to Navajo culture in the guise of a lively story. A must-read when crossing the Navajo Nation.

Desert Solitaire by Edward Abbey, published by Ballantine Books, ISBN 0345326490: the classic among the numerous books by Abbey, the rebel ranger, at once liberal and redneck. Abbey depicts his love of the desert with a fine sensibility. It's the perfect accompaniment for Arches and Canyonlands.

Centennial by James Michener, published by Fawcett Books, ISBN 0449214192: a remarkable book, even though it's not really about the Land of the Canyons. It's an absolutely fascinating saga of the west and a shock for those who have never read Michener.

Resources

National Parks & Monuments
   Arches N.P. (801) 259-8161
   Bryce Canyon N.P. (801) 834-5322
   Canyon de Chelly N.M. (602) 674-5436
   Canyonlands N.P/Island (801) 259-4712
   Canyonlands N.P/Needles (801) 259-4711
   Capitol Reef N.P. (801) 425-3791
   Cedar Breaks N.M. (801) 586-9451
   Glen Canyon N.R.A. (602) 645-8200
   Grand Staircase-Escalante N.M. (801) 826-4291
   Natural Bridges N.M. (801) 692-1234
   Pipe Spring N.M. (520) 643-7105
   Zion N.P. (801) 772-3256

State Parks
   Coral Pink Sand Dunes S.P. (801) 648-2800
   Dead Horse Point S.P. (801) 259-2614
   Edge of the Cedars S.P. (801) 678-2238
   Goblin Valley S.P. (801) 564-3633
   Goosenecks S.P. (801) 678-2238
   Kodachrome Basin S.P. (801) 679-8562

Other Parks & Organizations
   Antelope Canyon Unit, Navajo P&R (520) 698-3347
   Escalante Interagency Visitor Center (801) 826-5499

Monument Valley Navajo Tribal Park (801) 727-3287
Navajo Parks and Recreation at Window Rock (602) 871-4941
Paria Canyon-Vermilion Cliffs Wilderness (801) 644-2672
Utah State Parks and Recreation (800) 322-3770
Utah Travel Council (801) 538-1030
B.L.M. of Moab (801) 259-8193
Moab Information Center (801) 259-8825
Canyonlands-North Travel region (800) 635-6622
Canyonlands-South Travel region (800) 574-4386
Color Country Travel region (800) 233-utah
Road Conditions (800) 492-2400
Hall's Crossing Ferry (801) 684-7000

Flights Over Canyonlands
Gene Boyle (Slickrock Air Guides) is based at the Moab airport and offers flights over the entire region. (801) 259-6216, fax (801) 259-2226. Being located close to the Island in the Sky district, he is best for flights over this area.

Paul Swanstrom (Mountain Flying Service) is based at the Monticello airport (435) 259-8050. He doesn't fly in summer. Best for flights over the Needles and the Maze. Paul can pick you up and deposit you close to the Visitor Center at the Needles.

Needles Outpost (801) 979-4007: the accommodating owners of the Needles Outpost can arrange a flight directly for you. Don't hesitate to go there to talk with them and take advantage of their food and beverage service as well.

Equipment for the Narrows of the Virgin and the Subway
Zion Adventure, located right in front of the Zion Canyon Campground in Springdale (801) 772-1001, can equip you and give you directions for your forays into local canyons. They rent a complete line including dry suits, neoprene wet suits and other canyoneering equipment.

Antelope Canyon Concessionaires
Lake Powell Jeep Tours (520) 645-5501
Antelope Canyons Tours, Roger Ekis, (520) 645-8579

4x4 Rentals in Moab
Thrifty Car Rental (801) 259-7317
Slickrock 4X4 Rentals (435) 259-5678 or (888) 259-5337
Farabee's Jeep Rentals (801) 259-7494

About the Author

Born in Paris and based in Los Angeles, Laurent Martrès is President of Graphie Intl', Inc., a software and multimedia consulting and publishing firm he founded in 1982. He sits on the Board of Directors of several other software companies, including ASD Software, Inc. and Alsyd Corp. Laurent has spent a large amount of time criss-crossing the planet—and in particular the American West—on roads, 4x4 trails, footpaths and horse trails. He wrote this guide so others could benefit from his experience. Laurent also serves as a moderator of Compuserve's Photography Forum. As a photographer, he prefers the 6x4.5 medium format and Velvia transparency film.